Praise for *Rediscover*

"This book speaks the truth. We do live in a musical universe – simple as a Mozart sonata and deep as a Bach fugue. In sharing the song of his everyday life, Scott illuminates the divine harmony in the world and, in so doing, the music inside us all."

~ **Richard Merrick**, Independent Researcher,
Digital Media Entrepreneur, and Author of the Book
Interference: A Grand Scientific Musical Theory

"Scott Leuthold not only understands the process of transformation and spiritual awaking, he lives it and shares from his depth of experience! In both practical and poetic ways this wonderful book provides powerful insights and guidance for the process of reconnecting with the spirit and spark of life."

~ **Jonathan Ellerby PhD**, author of the best-selling
Return to the Sacred: Ancient Pathways to Spiritual Awakening,
CEO of the Tao Center for Inspired Living

"Rediscovering Your Divine Music is a rich and wonderful read, a true resource that encourages the reader to dive into the depths of what is truly important in life. Scott Leuthold's willingness to reflect upon his own spiritual journey by holding up the great seeds of universal truth is an invitation for all of us to embrace our time on earth with open-heartedness. What are the the cycles of life? What does it mean to live with full expression? How do I navigate the complexity of my own life? What is my unique gift? These are the questions that Scott addresses in his book. Pull out the hammock, make a cup of tea and settle in for an engaging read!"

~ **Lisa Redstone** M.A.;
Spiritual Services Provider, Teacher and Healer

"Can you learn from another's journey, can another's experiences influence your daily life, and can another's perspective of self-realization support you to realize within your Self that you will find your answers? Scott Leuthold's "Rediscovering Your Divine Music" is not only a practical step-by-step manual to show you how to connect to your inner divine harmony, his book is a gift which gives you the guidance to go inside your Self to find all the answers to the questions you have been asking. I highly recommend reading Scott's personal journey of transformation. This book will transform your life."

~ **Sherry Anshara**, Founder,
QuantumPathic Center of Consciousness

"Rediscovering Your Divine Music is a very personal, touching, and heartfelt expression of how to connect and deal with extraordinary events in your life – how music can be a synchronistic savior just when you need it.

I always believed that music is a 'great friend' who is always there for you, and this is exemplified by Scott throughout his book by pointing out the many inherent qualities of music that support the mind and soul. Balanced by his knowledge of resonance and nature, it doubles as a therapeutic manual on how to deal with your world and finding a sense of 'inner-peace' through the nature of music.

A beautifully written story and an expressive poetic journey into the union of mind, music and nature."

~ **Stuart Mitchell**, World-renown Classical Composer of *Seven Wonders Suite for Orchestra*, *The Rosslyn Motet*, and *DNA Variations*, Recognized Cymatics researcher of the Rosslyn Chapel, Scotland.

Pat

A gift for you.
May my book
bring light into
your life and
love into your
heart.

[signature]

REDISCOVERING YOUR DIVINE MUSIC

FINDING HARMONY & BALANCE THROUGH INNER PEACE

SCOTT C. LEUTHOLD

TOKEN ROCK, INC.
www.tokenrock.com

TOKEN ROCK, INC.

Published and distributed in the United States by: Token Rock, Inc. Find us online at: www.tokenrock.com. For information address: c/o Token Rock, Inc. 20165 N. 67th Avenue, 122A-187, Glendale, Arizona 85308

Book and Cover Design: Scott C. Leuthold
Cover Photograph: ©2010 Scott C. Leuthold

The author of this book does not dispense medical advice or prescribe the use of any technique as a form of treatment for physical, emotional, or medical problems without the advice of a physician, either directly or indirectly. The intent of the author is only to offer general information for the purpose of supporting you along your path of life toward emotional and spiritual wellness. The author and publisher assume no responsibility for your actions in the event you use any information herin for yourself.

ISBN: 978-0-9832896-7-8 (PB)
978-0-9832896-4-7 (Ebook)

First edition: September, 2011

Printed in the United States of America.

Library of Congress Control Number: 2011920838

For my father,

JAMES STEVEN LEUTHOLD

In your passing, you've given me the
ultimate gift of life.

I am forever grateful.

And for

CARRIE-ANNE

Your beauty, grace, and
divine presence have been my inspiration.
Your words have helped me open my mind
to so many possibilities.

Contents

"Each more melodious note I hear
Brings this reproach to me,
That I alone afford the ear,
Who would the music be."

~ Henry David Thoreau

A MEDITATION

The wind blows through the quivering needles of the mighty pine. Waving and blowing in the breeze, the tree sways to Nature's music. Its energy flows harmoniously with its surroundings. As the breeze travels down the canyon walls, the dust of the Earth swirls like the resonating tone of a twinkling chime. The dust dissipates and settles on ramparts below. Flowing effortlessly, the breeze rides a current of energy to the canyon floor. As it reaches the flowing stream, it caresses the sparkling caps of rushing water where sunlight dances on the rippling waves. Like a trio of a cappella vocalists, wind, water, and light unite; they are one.

As the breeze continues its journey through the pristine canyon it reaches you, as you sit still and silent upon an exposed escarpment. The cool breeze penetrates the depths of your soul. Nature's divine music whispers across your ears. Like the tree perched atop the canyon cliff miles away, your body waves in harmony with the energy flowing in and out of your very being. The warm rays of the mighty Sun comfort you on your journey to oneness. The singing birds welcome you to the choir. You are one with all the energy that surrounds you. Silently you repeat, "I am the energy. I am connected with my melody. I am peace. I am love."

Your connection to Self and the discovery of your own divine music within resonates outward, and twists into infinite unity with the energy surrounding you. You are one with all that was, all that is, and all that shall be. This is your destiny! It is the destiny of all things seen and unseen. United as one, we are the energy of the tree, the dust, and the flowing stream. We are the energy, and the energy is God.

INTRODUCTION

"The music plays. Listen and you shall hear."
~ SC Leuthold

These words speak volumes, yet what do they truly mean? As you will discover through reading *Rediscovering Your Divine Music*, music plays a more profound, prominent role in our lives than we can even begin to understand.

My personal quest has been to come to some sort of an understanding of who I am in this reality, and what purpose I have for being here. Through this experience of rediscovering myself and my connection to the harmony of all things I have spent a great deal of time in deep contemplation; I have philosophized with many colleagues on the subject, and I have often arrived at what I felt might be reasonable perspectives. As time went on, I came to understand that we are here for the journey and not the destination. We are here to learn and grow alongside our friends and family, spiritual beings that have likely shared with us the journey of many lifetimes. Above all else, *we all are one* is the message I wish you to take from this book.

The Melody

Through my own journey of self-discovery,

I have found one thing that remains profoundly true: There is a music that plays, regardless if you hear it or not. It is the music of Nature, the music of substance and void, the melody of infinity and immediacy. It is the tune of accomplishment and failure, organized systems and chaos, fear and love, prosperity and poverty, friend and foe, matter and antimatter. These things—everything we think we understand and have yet to discover—are instruments, harmoniously playing their divine piece of the grand music.

We, like everything else, are a part of that company of instruments. We, like everything else, play in tune with this divine music. However, as we enter this reality for some reason or another, we are stripped of our knowledge of this truth. As we grow into our physical bodies and mature, we are attracted further and further away from this truth until one day, many of us are no longer emotionally connected to it at all. We are still energy and our music still plays, yet the melody is muffled and muted until it can no longer be heard.

Our western society has become focused upon outward desires and has lost touch with personal worth replacing it with material and financial gain. The onslaught of commercialism, relentless exposure to negative media, the dependence upon external sources of healing, and the deterioration of our educational system have significantly diminished the focus on individual creativity as well as dampened the full expression of the innate power, unity, peace, and love that resides within.

Our natural power dramatically declines when the harmony between the Self and the divine is lost. While growing up most of us have been programmed by many disruptive influences from varied sources, including social institutions, family beliefs, and peer pressure, and this programming can adversely influence an entire lifetime.

There was a time when I felt I knew everything. Then one day, I discovered that what I believed might not actually be so. *Maybe what I believe to be true isn't true at all*, I pondered. *Maybe those around me know more, or maybe their beliefs should be accepted as my own.* As I matured further into my life, I again entered a new realization. I began to consider (and eventually decided) that everything I believed was, in fact, my reality. What I believed to be true was, in fact, true... *for me*. And what others believed to be true was, in fact, true... *for them.*

This book is about that journey of self-discovery and my own experiences that have led to a new way of thinking—a mindset that has changed everything in my life. It is about my own rediscovery of the divine music that I am, and my harmonious melody that brilliantly resonates with all that is and ever will be.

Through this book, you too may come to understand how your energy flows. You too may begin to hear the faint tune that is divinity within your own Self. And if you are ready, you too will venture down your own path of self-discovery. If you allow it to, this path will lead to a rediscovery of the music that you have always been. The universal language of all that is will play loudly within you from the depths of your soul. And when this music begins to be heard by your own ears, it will resonate with all you wish to have present in your life, and in harmony it will be.

Like the wings of the butterfly rippling waves of energy into the abyss, your music will send waves across the vast sea. And like the predictable tides, that energy will return home to your own shores and lap along the sands of your own reality. With it will come harmony with the world and everything you have always hoped to experience.

"I went to the woods because I wished to live deliberately, to front only the essential facts of life, and see if I could not learn what it had to teach, and not, when I came to die, discover that I had not lived."

~ Henry David Thoreau

The words of Henry David Thoreau, Ralph Waldo Emerson, and John Muir rang profoundly true for me when I was first exposed to them in my late teens.

Their literary mastery relating the natural world to a divine music left me with a new outlook on my existence. Reading the words submersed my mind in the experience of places like Walden Pond and the mighty Sierras, and in doing so, allowed new perspectives to take shape. My connection to Nature became a cornerstone of my life, and I tried to share in the experience as often as I could.

However, as I matured, the complexities of the societal world complicated things. With the multitude of decisions to make, I found there to be a separation between how I felt when I spent time in Nature, and my day-to-day experiences of stress, discontentment, chaos, competition, and so forth.

In this book, I share insights on the relationship between the natural world that surrounds us and our individual experience within it. I have found, through my own path to self-awareness and personal growth, that when we strip away the belief systems, segregated societal differences, day-to-day personal interests and agendas, and seemingly separated lives, we are but one entity—not just as a species, but a oneness with all things.

It is with this realization that we can find the connection between what we experience in the solitude of Nature and our connection to our higher Self. There can be a deep sense of peace when journeying down a wilderness trail, and it is possible to find a similar peace in our day-to-day lives that comes from our journey inward.

There can be a comprehensive approach to connecting with our natural environment—but don't worry! This connection doesn't require that we regularly find ourselves in wilderness. *Rediscovering Your Divine Music* offers a perspective that props open the door to contemplate how we fit into this grand, complex system. Through my own journey of exploring its inner workings, intellectual discussions with a wide range of experts, and philosophical conversations with individuals from all walks of life, I have found a sense of peace and gratitude from the knowledge I've gained. With a formulated understanding, I have discovered that the music of Nature has no beginning and no end. It is everywhere—from the birth of stars in deep space to our own thoughts, feelings, and emotions. And even more astonishing is the notion that there is no division between them. Everything—and I mean everything—is one grand symphony. It all plays in harmony, simultaneously and infinitely. The connection to Nature we find in wilderness can be found anywhere. Nature's music plays in everything and anything man has created, from the dawn of our existence.

My own journey has been to not only understand this concept, but also why it is this way. How and why does this happen? Why have I been given conscious thought in and amongst this experience to contemplate it at all? And when I contemplate its workings and formulate a perspective, how does that affect my experience? Or, even better yet, how do my thoughts about it affect the grand music; this miraculous experience we call life?

These questions have led me to explore any possibility that has been placed before me. Some I have accepted as real possibilities, while others I have set aside. I've not denied anything, but rather I have simply kept an open mind to what may be presented going forward. I have learned not to simply accept a concept just because it was written or spoken, understanding that anything that has been passed down through generations could simply be individual perspective, stories spun for personal gain. My quest has been to find my own truth and a life balance in this dualistic system we call home.

"Traveling to the distant corners of the world
in search of profound experience
affords us the opportunity to journey inward.

And on that journey we discover
that we needed not travel beyond our Self
to find our truth."

~ SC Leuthold

Chapter 1

AN AWAKENING

The Beginning of My Future

It wasn't until I experienced hardship in my life that I awakened to the reality that my role within this world was more profound, more definite than I had come to understand.

If you are among the many who have or are currently experiencing a revived sense of self-awareness or personal empowerment, or those who are, perhaps, questioning their reality and have embarked on a quest for knowledge and answers to life's questions, the transition quite possibly blossomed from the bud of a revelation caused by an experience that shook the very foundation in which you have built your life.

The cause really doesn't matter. It could have

been the death of a loved one or close friend, the failure of a long-held relationship, the collapse of a business and a loss of life's work, a dwindling nest egg, personal health issues, endless relentless limitations in life, or what have you. Maybe even just a simple shift in your thinking or an expansion of your awareness. No matter what it was, it has inspired you and you have discovered a light flickering within. Regardless of how faint or bright that light may illuminate, it still glows nonetheless. For many, that soft golden light enchants our very being to the depths of our souls, and here the light penetrates the darkness. It is in that darkness where we will find the answers we seek—our own answers. It is here that we shall explore new vibrations of time and timelessness. It is here that we shall challenge our beliefs. This is the place where we shall speak to the unknown and listen intently for our divine Self to respond.

My Father's Departure

A profound experience such as this is precisely what led me down my path to a spiritual awakening on a quest for knowledge.

It was a warm evening in the summer of 1998. I had been fumbling around the local hardware store, checking off a list of miscellaneous items to purchase. My wife and I had just taken possession of a new home in a small mountain community on the edge of metropolitan Phoenix, and we were moving in the next morning. As we browsed the aisles, my cellular telephone rang. It was my brother calling long distance from Wisconsin. He reluctantly revealed to me that my father had suddenly passed away. He had experienced a brain aneurism, and like a gust of sudden breeze that rushes through and quickly dissipates, he was gone from this reality. My reaction was one of sheer and utter disbelief. I was stunned and deeply saddened by the news.

My father and I admittedly did not entertain much of a relationship for a significant part of my childhood. It wasn't until my early twenties, after my wedding to my first wife, that Dad and I began to communicate with any regularity.

My mother and father divorced when I was in fourth grade. This event effectively split our family in two. My sister and I were relocated with my mother into town. My older brother, being of age to make his own decision for his future, opted to remain with my father. Dad made a number of attempts to keep a visitation schedule after the move, but as time went on, the visits became less frequent.

Little more than a year later, my mother and stepfather decided to relocate our new family to a community about a half-hour drive from where my father lived. We settled in to life in this new environment and began to make new friends. Due to the drive, my father's visits became few and far between.

Then, no more than a school year later, we were

once again relocated, this time more than three hours away from my father. Though Dad still visited my sister and me, this broader distance between us resulted in a deep void in our personal relationship. Our visits with Dad generally occurred only when my mother transported us back to our hometown to see him.

I spent my teens in western Wisconsin and after I graduated high school, my mom and stepfather decided once again to make a major move. This time, they relocated much further from our hometown—all the way to Arizona. Now age 18, I had the opportunity to do anything I wished at the time; but wanting to move west, I chose to follow them to Phoenix. Though I quickly became embedded in the local culture, this move was certain death for my relationship with Dad. As I moved into adulthood, my dad and I had almost no remaining relationship.

In my early twenties, I met my first wife. When we decided to get married, I invited Dad to the wedding and he and his wife attended. It was the first time I had seen him in a number of years. With the wedding planning, the ceremony, and the subsequent honeymoon to keep me busy, the visit with him was short. It would be another four years before he and I would rekindle our relationship one-on-one.

In the summer of 1997, seventeen years after my parents divorced, I decided it was time to work toward a new relationship with my father. My wife and I flew to Wisconsin, where he had lived all of his life. He had invited us to stay with him at his home. I wasn't quite sure how the visit would go, but when we arrived, my father and I hugged each other. Feelings I had apparently held deep within me came to the surface, and I cried in his arms.

From that moment forward, a new relationship blossomed between the two of us. We called each other on the phone, sent holiday greetings and gifts, and shared our lives as much as possible. The following summer, my wife and I made another trip to Wisconsin to spend time with him. It was a truly memorable experience I will never forget. Then, only a month after our return home to Arizona, that fateful phone call came with the news that he was gone.

I felt it necessary to stand before the hundreds of people who attended his funeral and share my story. I expressed to the silent, somber crowd that I had come to realize there are always lessons to be learned in life. I shared how my father and I had been separated, had lived our lives apart for so many years, and—only a year before his transition—had rekindled our relationship. I expressed how important it had become to me, through this profound experience, that we find a way to overcome differences and seek resolution to adversities with those whom we cherish in our lives.

After the funeral, I was walking down the back staircase of St. John's Catholic Church to the basement, where a number of people had gathered before the procession. On my way down, a gentleman stopped me to introduce himself. He shared with me how inspired he was by the words I had spoken behind the podium. He told me he and his son had been having some serious relationship issues and were not on speaking terms. He expressed to me that he had been enlightened with a new perspective and was going to approach his son in a new, more open and understanding way. Though he shared with me that my words had affected him in such a way, the reality was, his words had a profound effect on me. I came to realize that although I had been very nervous about standing before such a large crowd and sharing my personal intimate experiences openly and candidly, the act was inspiring to both me and this gentleman standing before me.

When I returned home to Arizona after the funeral, my perspective on life had changed. For the next few years, my father's death began to shape my perspective on life. I began to ask deep questions about my own life and happiness. I questioned if my father had been happy with his life. Though I would not come to formulate a perspective on my dad's life for some years to come, his death was certainly the catalyst for change in my own life. Through his death, my dad allowed me a new perspective—one by which my life has since been lived.

My Awakening Begins

Once we are offered a glimpse into a deeper, more profound sense of being, our lives are likely never to be the same again. My father's transition was the glimpse for me. It was the source of the questioning, the certainty and uncertainty, and the spark of the flickering light. The experience led me to dig deep within myself to make attempts to discover who I was, who I wanted to be, and the path for which I would need to travel to reach the source… my divine Self.

I began to spend time alone, hiking the mountain peaks and canyons near my home. There really is no better way to travel within than to spend time in solitude. Connecting to Self while experiencing Nature in all its grandeur has a way of touching the soul unlike any other experience. Doing so allows us to resonate harmoniously with the vibration. It gives each of us an opportunity to listen for the divine music of Nature and, in a sense, get back in sync with the source.

On several occasions, I found myself perched atop mountain peaks in meditation, with that as my primary purpose. I would sit there, propped up on a boulder, gazing out to the horizon. The cool breeze would caress my cheeks and ears. I would enter such a deep meditative state that time would pass by remarkably fast.

I would spend much of my time alone in deep thought, asking myself difficult questions, contemplating my life, my relationships, my beliefs, my perspectives on my reality, and my place within this remarkable world. I would envision my life the way I wanted it to be, making lists in my head of the steps I needed to take in order to realize that vision. I would express appreciation for my accomplishments and myself, and even recognize the difficult lessons I had already endured.

On my one-day adventures, I would just drive until I felt my intuition tell me I should stop. Often, these experiences would lead me to locales that offered no trails. Bushwhacking and boulder hopping were the norm, and that was perfectly fine with me. Solitude was my desire, and that is exactly what I found—in great abundance, free for the taking.

One Saturday morning, I discovered a very special place I lovingly came to refer to as "My Secret Canyon." Though accessing the canyon was fairly difficult and even treacherous at times—with crossings of the Salt River, a trek over rolling desert foothills, and constant dealings with Cats Claw bushes—once within the canyon, I was offered peace and solitude that was only to be shared with the wildlife that called this place their home. The difficulty in accessing the canyon made it an ideal place to be alone. No trail, no people. I hiked as far back into the canyon as time would allow. I'd boulder to the top of a jutting ridge on a dogleg, and sit overlooking the canyon walls and floor. I felt as though I were a part of the ecosystem that allowed me to truly know the place. Because I asked nothing of the canyon other than to be a part of it for a short time, I felt that the place opened up to me—or even more likely, that I allowed myself to open up to it. The canyon shared a peace and serenity that I had not been exposed to very often in my life prior. I had had many experiences in Nature in my youth, but this was different. I was alone, dependent only on myself and a trust in the unity of this astounding place and me. I experienced there a true sense of harmony between my own melody and that of the natural world. My usual perch, a point on a sharp curve, was high above the canyon floor. It was a perfect position to receive the energy of the cool breeze flowing through, yet it allowed me to bask in the rays of sunlight. There, I spent a great deal of the time contemplating life, seeking to simplify my perspectives by removing any so-called complications I had been experiencing.

Solitude is one of the primary tools available to each of us for getting in touch with our higher Self. It is the raw sense of Nature that brings us back to our roots, and the basic elements of our existence. It is something each and every one of us inherits upon our arrival to this reality, yet I suspect it is a tool that is seldom used effectively.

I only paid two more visits to My Secret Canyon after that first experience. I moved on to new locations, reciprocating to the canyon the peace it had afforded to me.

The following spring, I hiked on a number of occasions to the top of the many peaks in the McDowell

Mountains near my home at the time. Sitting atop one of the highest peaks in the range, I found myself in yet another moment of deep contemplation. My body felt deeply planted to the surface of the giant boulder upon which I was propped. It was a cool, crisp morning. The sky was bright blue with a purple hue along the horizon. The auburn rays of the morning sunrise were cresting over the distant Mazatzal mountain range on the eastern slope of the Verde River valley. I had been fumbling my hands around beside me and gripped a small basalt stone without much consideration of it. My mind was elsewhere in deep thought and contemplation. With the stone in hand, I committed to find happiness from within. I dedicated myself to take a stand for my own life and make any changes necessary to achieve my goal of realizing true happiness from within. In that moment, I experienced such a range of emotions: hope, fear of the unknown, selfishness, love for myself, guilt for what I felt I would need to do that would affect others around me, resentment for the weakness I had experienced that led me down the path I had been on, hesitation and excitement. It all came at once. One thing was certain: I felt more alive in that moment than I had felt in a long time. And it was that feeling that drove me to take decisive action.

I think most people fear the unknown, whether we admit it or not. In fact, it seems fair to say that fear itself is the result of not knowing. We concern ourselves with the guilt of making a change that will produce unknown results. Who might I hurt? What will they think of me? How will I survive? I'm not sure it really matters what anyone thinks, but it certainly does have an impact on our sense of guilt. When I look back now with the knowledge I have gained since that moment, I can appreciate all the emotions I had felt simply as belief systems that I am totally and completely in control of. But at the time, I was only focused on one thing: change.

It seems that when we finally come to grips with what we really desire, it takes a literal closing of the eyes and a blind step forward into the abyss. Far too often, we fear that we will plummet to our death rather than soar like a dove. Saying we want to truly live life, and actually doing it, are two very definitive steps in the process. What it comes down to is faith. To be more precise, faith in ourselves, faith in the fact that we are the creator of our own reality, faith that we are one with a higher power and that this source, this master, or whatever you wish to call it, wants for you what you ultimately want for yourself—pure, unwavering love and true happiness.

At that time, I felt so strapped into my life. The visual that came to me was my physical body lying in a web of muscle tissue fused to my skin. The muscle mass held me down to every aspect of my current life. I felt like I couldn't breathe. It seemed like I couldn't even lift my head to look around. I needed to break free, and for that to happen, the muscle mass holding me down would need to tear. I knew there would be pain and suffering, and that healing would ultimately need to take place. I knew some of that healing would likely take a long time for those around me, but it just had to happen. It wasn't for years to come that I would learn about becoming a conscious creator and what that meant in my life, but I know now, and I share this with you. In that very moment, I became a conscious creator of my own reality. I took control. I was handed the reins and became the director of the production called Scott's Life. I was now empowered, and with that empowerment and strength came a flow of energy through me that I had never felt before... and this was just the beginning.

(For further reading, my personal journal entry written about this experience dated August 2002 can be found in the back of this book.)

The Spark of New Light

So, this is what my father's transition out of this reality created for me: opportunity, not loss. Not a mountain of pain, but a mountain to climb, for which I could give myself a 360-degree view of the world outside of what was right in front of me.

All too often, I encounter individuals who have experienced significant and abrupt changes in their lives, and rather than seize the opportunity to embrace change, they sandbag walls in their minds to hold back the rushing current in a feeble attempt to hold on to their existing belief systems. Years pass, and their lives remain stuck in the relentless and repeating program of pain and suffering behind the psychological barriers they have constructed in their minds and hearts. This limits growth and learning, and squelches the natural expanding of awareness and consciousness. Their practices of holding back change become second nature until one day, they feel as though the pain and suffering is no longer something they can avoid or release. I am here to tell you that you can let it go!

There is a candle located in the deep, dark corner of your consciousness, and upon its wick is an eternal flickering flame. It is simply a choice to be made by you and only you, a choice to navigate the dusty spaces of the mind to locate that flame. There is no rule that states you can't awaken your truth, no matter how difficult it may seem or how old or young you may be.

One of the finest analogies I have ever heard with regard to achieving one's goals is this. And I should add that it speaks volumes in relationship to finding that flame, and using it to walk the path of individual truth.

Imagine yourself sitting behind the wheel of your vehicle at night. You turn the key, and the spark ignites the engine. The headlights illuminate the immediate space in front of you. Through the windshield, you can see a clear path to follow, but the light only illuminates the space so far in front of you. Beyond the reach of that light, darkness shrouds the path. Knowing full well that the headlights will only enlighten the immediate space in front of the car, you drive on. Heading to another community across the countryside, you advance, believing with little doubt that you will make it to your destination safe and sound. You see, the headlights provide enough distance before you to move forward in every moment of your journey. This is also true with your discovery of the flickering flame. Do what is necessary to rise up from the deep rut you may have found yourself in. Grip that eternal light in the palm of your hand. Raise your hand into the darkness before you. Allow it to penetrate that darkness, and take your first step toward it. As you move forward, so will the light, leading the way to who you truly are.

Farewell Lu Lu

My grandmother transitioned out of my reality not many years after my father passed. Lu Lu, as many of my extended family members so affectionately called her, was a warm and loving woman. My mother's mother, she spent the last years of her existence here being taken care of by my mom and stepfather. Toward the end of her life, our family decided to move her to a care center out in the country in northeast Arizona. When she was moved to the facility about three and a half hours from my home, I visited her on only a few occasions. On one occasion, my mother asked me if I would attempt to convince her to take a shower. Apparently, she was in a state-of-mind where she was experiencing some pain stemming from her advanced age; perhaps she was coming to grips with the final moments of her life.

My wife Carrie-Anne and I traveled to visit her with our sons that weekend. Unbeknownst to me at the time, it would be the last time I would see or speak to her before she passed, and that time with her was a very profound experience for me. Upon our arrival, Carrie-Anne, the boys, and I all entered her room and chatted with her for a while. She looked frail, and knowing her so well, I presumed she wasn't comfortable with her appearance. She had always been a beautiful woman, quite comfortable throughout my lifetime taking credit for any good looks our family possessed. Her comments of this nature always generated smiles and chuckles from the family.

After a while, Carrie-Anne offered to take the boys out front of the facility so I could spend time alone with my grandmother. This time alone with her was almost foreign to me. Though Lu Lu and I had shared many moments in life alone together, this was different. When I was in high school, I spent a few summers living with her and my grandpa in the resort community of Fish Creek in Door County, Wisconsin. I lived with them in the summers while I worked on the beach at the local state park. At that time, our roles were more or less like a parent/child relationship. My grandmother took good care of me, even though I suspect that I was a bit of a challenge to deal with back then.

But that was many years earlier, and now Lu Lu's body had been deteriorating for some time. The signs were certainly pointing to the end of the road for her experience. These signs created an awareness among her extended family, making it exceedingly important to reunite. One by one, my aunts, uncles, and cousins made their pilgrimage to Arizona from around the country. Over a few short weeks, my grandmother was blessed to enjoy the one thing in her life that she loved and valued the most: her family.

Now, though, my grandmother was lying in a hospital bed with the defused window light cast upon her face and arms. Out the window, the high desert pinion pines studded the land as far as the eye could see. The window was cracked, and the entering breeze enticed the sheer window curtains to dance and flutter. Her eyes were closed. I approached her and sat on the bed beside her and gripped her frail hand. Her skin was dry and flaked from her forehead to her cheeks and clear down to her arms. I asked her if she would like me to rub lotion into her skin to moisten it. She nodded in agreement. I slowly and tenderly caressed her face, bringing color back with every stroke. She seemed to respond with satisfaction. I sat with her for quite a while, silently holding her hand. Then I asked her if she might make the effort to rise from the bed and shower. She really had no interest, but my offering to help her changed her mind. I don't think she was comfortable with the facility staff managing this very private process. I imagine there is a loss of dignity in having one's fragile, aged body exposed to a non-relative for the simple task of cleansing.

I helped her rise from the bed and sit in a wheel

chair. The male facility staff person walked her chair to the adjacent bathroom. We stood her, and I walked her to the shower and assisted in undressing her. For some reason, I felt uncomfortable looking at her. I felt I was invading her privacy. Looking back, it seems I had a fear to overcome, and having done so back then would have been more dignified for her than having anyone assisting me. Regardless, I sensed she appreciated my presence and felt a sense of safety and peace of mind because I was there.

After her shower, I dressed her and helped her back into bed. I sat beside her and again applied lotion to her face and hands. We discussed a number of subjects and seemed to connect much more in the heart than I had ever before with her. I am not sure if it was my gut feeling about how much time she had left to share, or if it was simply the raw human emotion that one experiences when all else in the world is stripped away, leaving only the natural process of life and our spiritual connection to it. Either way, a very spiritual bond was made in that moment for me. When I finished applying lotion, I kissed her on the forehead, shared my love with her, and departed. It was the last time we spoke.

Lu Lu's departure was yet another pivotal experience for me that helped me put life into perspective. I was able to see how the body does not make the person—or, to state it more appropriately, "*our human existence does not sum up the essence of our spirit*." This was the first time in my life that I was given an opportunity to be close and connect with an individual who was being faced with the unavoidable end of their current lifetime. I wondered how my grandmother felt about being faced with such an experience. In her case, I am not so sure she was ready to die. In fact, I believe on the day I sat at her bedside, she had not yet accepted it. Again, in retrospect, if I had been experiencing those moments with her today, I would have been more equipped to comfort her, but this life is not about living with regret. Life is about experience, forgiveness, and ultimately release, and this was one experience that left me profoundly grateful.

The experiences of my father and grandmother's transitions were moments in life that I embraced as opportunities. In those moments, I was faced with the acceptance that there are things in life I simply *don't know* that I don't know. You see, there are things *we know* we know, such as the foods we like, how to tie our shoes, and so on. There are things *we know* we don't know, for instance, I know that I do not have any idea how to fly an airplane (although I would like to learn). And then, there are things we *don't know that we don't know*. These things are part of our subconscious mind—the things we may or may not have an opportunity in this lifetime to come to understand. When we are offered opportunities to learn, especially knowledge that can affect our very being; we need to embrace them with a dedicated focus on observing our actions, our behaviors, and our emotions to formulate a position about that experience. Then, if it feels right to do so, we can forgive and release it. These moments are why we are here. They are the ingredients of life experience that shape our perspectives and, in turn, allow us opportunities to expand consciousness and awaken to our own truth.

Understanding the Awakening Process

The concept of the term *awakening* to me is one that requires an open mind. Why? Because becoming fully conscious of one's Self means that one's existence is entirely their responsibility, not anything or anyone elses. Opening our minds to what we may be capable of (and all that comes with it) opens the door to a shift in our reality.

Awakening is a term that, to me, describes the shift from complacency, lack of knowledge, and an acceptance that things are not within our own control, to an existence where we become completely self-aware, self-empowered, and achieve a *sense* of balance with all things. It is the voluntary decision to become a conscious creator of our own lives.

Many have yet to awaken to this reality, yet those who are on the path to an awakening must understand that it is not a destination that one necessarily eventually *reaches*, but rather an ongoing journey full of experiences. The good news is that we can learn from these experiences until we finally transition away from this reality.

It has become a common understanding among the scientific community that the world, including humans, presents itself in the form of energy. Energy is simply vibrational frequency—or, more appropriately put, a *universal music*. The walls of our homes, the leaves on the trees, animals, water, matter and anti-matter, your thoughts, your feelings, sound, and the colors that make up the spectrum of light—everything is music.

The frequency at which Earth's energy vibrates is 7.8 Hz, albeit some believe this is changing. Our human form resonates at the same frequency as that of Earth. When we choose to become awakened in our own life, we are simply selecting a path that may eventually lead us to a balance of mind, body, and soul in harmony with all things.

Through this process, we find that we can achieve great things. We can choose to be happy, healthy, and full of life. We can choose our experiences and our emotional responses to those experiences. We begin to understand that we need not hold on to beliefs we once held so dear if, in fact, these beliefs no longer ring true to us.

Oftentimes, those who head down this path of awakening find that it frees them from pain, suffering, depression, guilt, lack, fear, and stress, and these negative rhythms are replaced with rhythms that are harmonious, resonating an energy that is magnetic. It's simple, really: Good things happen when we are free from the limitations we place on ourselves due to the belief that they are unavoidable. We are able to make clearer choices.

You may find yourself hungry for information, any information, related to finding your own truth about your existence. The more you read, the more you research, and the more you open your mind to any and all possibilities as to why we are here and why you have been given the opportunity to experience, the more you will find your true happiness in life. As a result, you will awaken to limitless possibilities in your own life and will feel the desire to pass on to others your happy, positive energy. You will feel you are beginning to know and love yourself enough to be able to know and love others.

Awakening is not always a subtle change in your life. It truly is a cleansing process—both physically and emotionally. Once you actually release beliefs you once held so dear, you may discover that others around you must make a choice to either adjust to the new you or not. You may be challenged by others' beliefs that they continue to hold dear. If this happens, it is okay. To achieve balance with all things, we must accept that others have choices to make in their own lives. You may feel a desire to share your freedom of limitations with them, and you will have every right to do so if it feels right to you. However, you must also realize that judgment is a belief system all the same. A focus on achieving balance with all things helps to release us from judgment because we find that we are all here for our own experience. Others may not understand your path. They may judge you. They may apply their belief systems on you...and they have every right to do so. The difference is that you now understand that you are free to release those judgments and relationships. You are even free to simply extend compassion for their experience. You can simply smile and reflect with the realization that everything is simply an experience, and you are nothing more than an observer.

The path to awakening is one that is about ***you***. It is a choice made by you to achieve inner growth, to find your own truth, and to live with a sense of balance that exists harmoniously with that outside of yourself. It is the realization that though we appear to be individuals independent of one another, we are really part of a whole —one collective consciousness.

Interestingly, this entire description of the concept of awakening is simply my own belief based on my own research, and my own personal choice to become self-empowered. It is important to understand that to choose the path to achieving balance, the balance itself comes from finding our own truth—whatever truth it is that rings true for each one of us—while making choices based on the understanding that all people and all things in this reality are one... and that they are all a part of you.

A Divine Balance

There was a place with morning sun
That kissed the hedgehogs one by one.

There was a place so free and wild
Like the innocent spirit of a newborn child.

There was a place of crystal dreams
With shadowed canyons and mountain streams.

There was a place where Nature sang
And one could walk where gardens hang.

There was a place I called my own
And built up walls with Nature's stone.

There was a place I'd forever scar
Its limits I knew not near or far.

This place had known no weight of me
Yet honored the growth of my rooting tree.

There was a place of clear blue skies
But now I've grown and hide my eyes.

The walls I've built now have no end
Its face I've cut may never mend.

But yet I grow, and throughout my life
I continue to cut with my scarring knife.

Until this place has lost its way
And Nature's melodies no longer play.

There was a place with morning sun
That kissed them goodbye one by one.

~ SC Leuthold

Chapter 2

ROLE PLAY

Identifying Our Self in Our Reality

I wrote this poem in my early twenties at a time in my life when I was first coming to grips with humanity's infliction on the environment. This was a very important issue to me at the time. It wasn't until later in life that I began to contemplate the distinguishing roles we play in this reality, both individually and as one collective consciousness. It became apparent to me that even though our purpose here may be to forgive what is presented before us and release ourselves from our strapping egos, we must also learn to respect our fellow man and the natural surroundings in which we reside. Why? Because the more we extend respect in the way we wish to be respected, the less we must ultimately forgive in order to achieve enlightenment.

Here, in this reality, we each play roles. These roles offer to each of us various paths to follow. Along the paths we choose, we are granted opportunities to learn and expand our awareness. Sometimes we make choices that result in outcomes that do not appeal to us or cause us to second guess. In those moments, we are in a position to decide if the choice generated the outcome we preferred.

Throughout our lifetimes, we are given an opportunity to make limitless choices. These are a direct reflection of how we present ourselves externally, and how we honestly view ourselves in our subconscious mind. These reflections present themselves, and when they do, we make choices. However, all too often, those choices are made without conviction. We make them based on the premise that we are individuals, beings separate from one another, entities entirely segregated from the natural environment that surrounds us. On the contrary, we are all that we see and do not see. We are all that we think and do not think with our complex minds. To make a choice without this understanding is to make a choice in haste. Knowledge gives us the power to make choices based on love and forgiveness. These attributes lead us back to our ultimate truth: the realization that we are one with the source now and forever. Any decision made outside of this knowing is made by our own egos, without question. For me, this has been a difficult concept to grasp.

The ego is tricky. At every juncture, it has

planned out for you how you will react. Unless we come to understand how the ego works, we will go about our day making choices based on attributes that may not ultimately benefit us or those we share this reality with. Our world has become a place where outward possessions are held in the highest value and regard. Commercialism and materialism are seeded in greed, lack, judgment, jealousy, and guilt—all of which are attributes of fear. The ego thrives on fear, and it isn't very difficult to see how the ego and fear together have formulated a society that has segregated our population in favor of material success at a cost of losing not just control, but also mutual respect.

It is easy to see how allowing the ego to take control has shaped our world, and how allowing that control to be lost has led to more of the same. The more our ego takes hold, the more we give away our control, and vice versa. This is what has ultimately led us to political wars, hate crimes, terrorism, rape, abuse of ourselves, others, and the environment, overpowering governments, dictatorships, many organized religions manipulating historical facts for personal gain, and so on. It is what has continuously sparked one of the world's most criminal oxymorons: the so-called "holy war."

But how can it be that we, as a collective entity, could have segregated ourselves so minutely from the oneness we once were to create war in defense of our spiritual beliefs? It is quite simple, really. We chose it based on fear that has been embedded in our subconscious minds from a time preceding our births in this lifetime. Once we arrived here, that fear was put center stage and nurtured into our adulthood by our own egos. And, as the ego is prone to systematically do, it will make choices based on fitting in with society and effectively following the crowd. Our egos create experiences to support the fear that drives it forward. This happens over and over again until one day, something happens that raises questions in the mind about the validity of the beliefs we hold dear.

Now, I would like to address that the event that raises these questions does not necessarily need to be a major catastrophe. Nevertheless, whatever the experience, it certainly will be pivotal. Mine was my father's passing as I mentioned earlier, but for others, it could be something that seems trivial on the surface. However, have no doubt that no matter how large or small it appears to be on the surface, the moment is as profound as any.

A New Path for Me

Once I finally made the choice to find true happiness from within, it was certainly not immediate. In fact, it is far from over for me. I focus on it as often as I can while still trying to function in my societal role as a partner, father, son, brother, friend, neighbor, and businessperson.

I have learned a great deal since that day on the mountain, and to be completely honest, many of the choices I have made since that time have largely been based on ego response. But I have made a concerted effort to recognize those choices, and whenever possible, I make new choices based on that recognition. There is nothing wrong with making mistakes. They are a natural characteristic of our existence here. This is how we learn. I should point out that to become enlightened, we do not necessarily have to change anything related to our current life path in society unless the choices we make along that path are based on ego. If choices are honestly made with forgiveness and love, then we need not create change. However, if we are not being honest with our Self, even for a moment, something likely needs to change.

Today, I have learned to simply forgive the experiences of the past that surface in my mind and release myself from their gripping hold. Each day is a new day, and in each moment of that day, we have opportunities to choose with the right attributes of forgiveness and love.

My life path led me to end a 13 year relationship when I was 32-years-old. I came to understand that the path I put myself on when I was just nineteen years old was not the right path for me. It took a tremendous amount of courage to make that change in my own life, but I finally chose it because I believed it was necessary for me to find my right path in life.

Meeting Someone New

As time went by, I began a new relationship with

a childhood friend. We spent almost three years together and became engaged, but in the end, the partnership didn't stand the test of time. At the time, not only was my ego still largely in control of my life, but I was also not equipped with the tools to recognize it.

The relationship, as it turned out, was not suitable for my life path. However, my choice to put our engagement on hold in favor of focusing on the relationship was, in large part, my own choice based on judgment. I felt as though my partner was not focused on the important aspects of the relationship, but in reality, her personality was simply not feeding my ego. *"I have needs, and those needs are not being met,"* my ego told me. The fact of the matter is, I was expecting more out of my partner than I should have been. Now, that doesn't mean that I should have remained in the relationship; however, that might have been the case if I could have released myself from my ego.

It is just as important to recognize that both parties must be conscious of ego control for a relationship or partnership to truly work. And frankly, an individual focused on forgiveness recognizes that no one is to blame because ultimately, we are all whole and complete. Only when we recognize at some point in our lives that our ego isn't who we truly are can we start making choices apart from it.

So for me, it was a case of cart before the horse. I was awakening to who I really am, but I hadn't started down the path necessary to expose me to the tools I needed to achieve my ultimate goal of true happiness from within—the tools of forgiveness, release, and love.

At the same time, I was reminded every morning when I brushed my teeth of my promise to myself on that mountaintop. In my medicine cabinet, I had always kept that rock I had gripped in my hand. Its daily presence was a wake-up call, and I could sense there was something wrong—something I needed to address. I had started to overcome my fears, but I certainly had not mastered the process. And to be honest, I still haven't today, although I am significantly better at the practice than I was back then. It was still a very difficult choice, and it left a deep pit in my stomach. But again, the choice was necessary. Our relationship had grown out of a fantasy of childhood friends reuniting after twenty-some years, and though it was truly romantic—like something out of a movie or a storybook—it wasn't ultimately a path that felt right for me.

I think one key learning experience for me in this lifetime has been to come to the realization that if we are not happy along our path, we can make choices to change it. Life may be complicated, but it isn't so restrictive that we are not allowed happiness. Another bit of knowledge I have gained is the understanding that happiness is not an outward journey; it truly is inward. Now, that isn't to say outward experiences do not influence inward happiness. It would be very difficult in this dualistic reality to achieve that without a great deal of focus and extensive conscious work. So, if there are definite outward experiences that do not suit us, it is completely realistic to make choices to change them. We must be in a place in our lives where we feel comfortable enough to focus on the inward Self. Oftentimes, this requires us to take ourselves out of stressful situations that keep us from finding peace and achieving clarity.

The end of that relationship was far from a victory, but it certainly was a choice in favor of my individual happiness. It wasn't a win against the ego, but all the same, it was an experience to learn from... and eventually I did. I want to stress the word *"eventually,"* because it is important to understand no one is perfect. We will learn from our choices when the time is right. If that revelation takes place years after an experience, it is just as effective as when it happened. We can always forgive ourselves and others, no matter how far in the past the experience may be, even if the individual we experienced it with is no longer here in this reality.

As will be discussed later in this book, even past-life experiences that may have had residual effects can be forgiven and released. That makes for quite the powerful tool for connecting to the higher Self. But even accessing this powerful enlightenment tool is a choice. To consciously choose a path toward enlightenment requires that we first come to some sort of understanding about who we are in this reality.

Hot on the Trail of My Identity

It wasn't until a friend of mine turned me on to a seminar program that I truly started to gain access to the tools in my long-forgotten life toolbox. A number of my artist friends had been involved in taking a course that, from my perspective, had opened the door to them becoming inspired enough to chase their life passions. I was quite inspired just witnessing them making these choices in their lives that sparked so much excitement. It was truly motivating. One had presented an idea to his boss for him to open a new design studio location for their firm that he would head up, and his boss had agreed. Another had decided to start his own photography business, and it was taking off. Yet another had completely overhauled her personality. In all honesty, I really wasn't a fan of her before, but now, she was amazingly receptive and warm-hearted.

At the time I was the acting creative director of a web development firm. I had hired my friend Stephen as a designer, and he decided to take the course, seeking some inspiration for himself. He returned with a decision to pursue his long-held dream of becoming an independent film director. Over the course of several months, I watched him leverage his home with a second mortgage, purchase all the necessary equipment, and start writing a script. Talk about a risk! When the script was complete and edited, he put together a team of professionals, and he produced a film. He submitted the film and actually received an independent film award for his work. I was stunned, to say the least. To this day, he still follows his passion and has won several awards for his films. In fact, he and his team have even been highlighted in several national news and entertainment magazines for their accomplishments.

My Turn to Shine

I had recently moved from my downtown bungalow to an investment property I owned on the far edge of the city. It was total culture shock moving that far from downtown, but being that my partner and I were no longer together, I decided to give it a try—it wasn't as though I needed to commute for my job, since I worked from home as a freelance designer.

I moved into the house in October that year and was scheduled to attend the workshop series the following January. I was ready to gain access to my own inspiration, and hoped the event would offer insights to me in the same way it had for many of my friends.

Living in this remote community of family households made for quite a lonely experience. I had rarely lived completely alone, and it was something I wasn't all that used to. I consider myself to be quite social, and even today, I feel as though there is a part of me that has not tapped into the power of being completely alone for extended periods of time. I love solitude, but I prefer it in smaller doses. I presume it would be a powerful growth experience for me, however, and it may one day lead me to a few extended solo expeditions. Aside from my dog, my social network lay completely online while I plugged away at design projects through out the day. On certain evenings of the week, I would have overnight parenting time with my son that often brought my experience back to center.

It wasn't long before I made a new and unexpected friend in the neighborhood. His name was Cameron, a 10-year-old boy from next door. Wintertime in the desert is a beautiful time of the year to open the windows and doors. I would work in my office, located in the front room of the house. One day, I received a knock on the door. Cameron introduced himself and mentioned that he liked the music I was listening to. He had just gotten home from school and was playing in front of his home when he heard my music. I invited him in to sit in my office while I worked. We chatted for quite a while, and then he left.

The next day, he returned for a second visit. I again invited him in. This time, he asked me if he could play my acoustic guitar that was standing in the corner of the room. Ironically (or maybe synergistically), I had received the guitar only weeks earlier as a birthday gift and had yet to learn to play it. Cameron, however, was amazing with the instrument. He played for me for at least an hour and then offered to teach me to play. At his young age, Cameron could play everything from Latin classical music to classic rock and modern grunge, and he was completely self-taught. I accepted his offer, and on future visits, he proceeded to teach me the cords.

It wasn't long before I noticed that Cameron's mother also worked from home, something not too difficult to figure out in a community where the majority of the residents commuted into the city for work. Most of the time during the day, it seemed we were the only two people home. As a single mom, Carrie-Anne worked as an interior designer for residential properties. It wasn't long before we also became friends, and since we had similar interests we began to take time out of our mid-week workdays to hike and play tennis. We developed a great friendship and had wonderful conversations about life and our philosophical perspectives.

One day, she emailed me and asked if I had ever explored my astrology, sending a link to an astrology website for me to read my in-depth monthly horoscope. After reading it, I was stunned. Almost everything the astrologer described was accurate, right down to the current day. It wasn't as though I was just coincidentally experiencing a few things. This horoscope was unbelievably accurate, so much so that I printed it and read it to my parents when they came to visit that week. Whether astrological charts and horoscopes are consistently accurate is sometimes questionable, but this one was dead-on. Their jaws dropped almost as much as mine had. The experience was eye-opening. Being of a more esoteric concept, I began to wonder what underlying power or energy was at play in my life. I began to wonder if there were other factors that led me to relocate.

Carrie-Anne shared with me that her previous partner, whom she had met a year earlier, had experienced a devastating car accident and passed away, leaving her single again. She, too, had been on a journey of self-discovery since that traumatic experience. The accident had left her with countless questions about life and her place within it. The transition of loved ones often became a focal point of our philosophical discussions. We would bounce ideas off one another, exchange books, and share web links. It was a special relationship in which we were both able to gain new knowledge and perspectives. With the growing power of our relationship, I wondered if there was any possibility that her past partner and my father were conspiring from a higher place to bring us together. Our lives seemed aligned in a unique way, unlike any one I had ever known—an alignment of inner perspectives.

Exposure to the Concept of Intuition

Along the way, Carrie-Anne also introduced me to intuitive readings. In fact, she introduced me to three different intuitive individuals over the course of a few months. The first was her Aunt Donna, a wonderful, warm-hearted woman with a soft-spoken Southern accent. Donna enlightened me with a great deal of information she picked up from my energy. She acted as a vehicle for me to talk with Lu Lu, and she shared with me some thoughts about what I might expect from my future. It was an eye-opening experience, being that I had never spoken with an intuitive previously—at least not that I knew of.

Then came a gentleman named Jon that Carrie-Anne had made friends with before we met. Though I was less comfortable with the reading with Jon, he gave me an opportunity to talk with my father. I gathered that he was well and in his current experience learning a great deal to apply to his next go-round in this reality. Jon also shared with me a remarkable bit of information that completely correlated with something Donna had shared with me about my future. It left me feeling very intrigued, considering that he and Donna had never met and my readings were both done in private.

A short time passed, and yet another aunt of Carrie-Anne's visited, this time from her father's side of the family. Aunt Judy was from the east coast. Her words were inspiring as well, and to my amazement she also shared with me a future scenario that resembled the ones mentioned in the readings from the other two intuitives. I was (and still am) convinced that there are energies within this reality that we have yet to truly understand. It would be another year before I would learn how to tap into my own intuition in a similar way to benefit my Self. Nonetheless, having three different people I had never met share with me almost identical views of my future convinced me that they must be on to something.

Since that time, others have relayed a similar vision for my future. Regardless if I pursued the future they each shared, I knew the capabilities they had each developed must be available to each of us if we so choose. For me, the experience also solidified my commitment to walking my path toward inner growth, self-empowerment, and a spiritual connection to my higher Self.

January rolled around quickly. Since I was scheduled for the weekend workshop, I asked Carrie-Anne if she would be interested in attending as well. She agreed and booked her ticket. The workshop was designed so that participants were supposed to partner with someone they didn't know, but since Carrie-Anne and I had only known one another for a couple months, we decided to work together. In some respects, this might have limited our development in the workshop, but it turned out to be an amazing experience. We were given a rare opportunity to get to know each other from the inside out in raw honesty; it was like *The Dating Game* meets my personal diary. If there could be a way for strangers to meet their ideal mate in life, something like this would surely be a winner.

During the weekend, we were asked to communicate with someone we were at odds with. I reluctantly contacted my ex-wife, and we talked on the phone. It was a touching moment for us both, and it helped me to realize that it is possible to heal our lives and forgive.

Carrie-Anne and I both walked away from the workshop deeply changed. The profound experience gave me a strength in myself that I had not felt since high school, yet I also felt I had been equipped to apply that strength and make good use of it. I was about to embark on my ultimate journey to create my life the way I had always wanted it to be.

Identifying Our Self

After that experience, Carrie-Anne and I both became enthralled with research on a wide variety of subjects. I feel fortunate to have had someone as vested in self-empowerment as I was at the time. We both devoured information. Carrie-Anne often delved deeper into certain subjects and shared new material with me, just as I did for her. It was extremely valuable to have someone to bounce ideas off of anytime I felt compelled to do so.

It makes so much sense to participate in group studies and book clubs or to find a friend to discuss philosophy with. A great deal of information can come from a variety of perspectives. From time-to-time, Carrie-Anne and I host Philosophy Night engagements at our home and invite a wide range of individuals to discuss perspectives. It can be a great social gathering, opening the door to new ideas. Communication is the source of knowledge, and sharing ideas leads the way. By communicating with others, we are able to open up to all possibilities and determine our own truths. From those truths, we are able to develop a perspective on our own existence in this reality, thus formulating a position of who we feel we are in relationship to those perspectives.

It is each of our responsibilities to find our own truths in this reality. No one else can do it for us, though many may attempt to manipulate our thinking to accept their truth as our own. It is important to communicate with others to receive new information, yet it is equally important to hold on to only the information that feels right. This helps to organize our perspectives as to who we are versus who we are not.

The process makes way for us to discover our Self along the path of life in each and every moment. Once we have achieved a sense of who we are *within* this reality, it can open the door to exploring who we are *without* this reality.

Fragment: Language Has Not the Power

*"Language has not the power to speak what love indites:
The Soul lies buried in the ink that writes."*

~ **John Clare**, 1950

Chapter 3

CHALLENGES AHEAD

Meeting and Beating Tough Moments in Life

That spring, Carrie-Anne and I moved in together, and just as things were going swimmingly, we experienced a great deal of turmoil. As it turned out, our two youngest boys didn't quite get along. They were caught up in what I will call an "altercation." The experience led my ex-wife to start what would become a three year court battle over child custody, and during the process, Carrie-Anne's ex-husband would throw in a few punches with an additional court battle from his side. We were hit from both sides, and it definitely affected our family life and our pocketbooks while challenging our thoughts and perspectives on life. It was a rough time, but interestingly enough, our quest for knowledge and the balance we were both so eager to create in our lives kept everyone in our family settled. My son's mother was successful in restricting him from coming to our home and being a part of our family.

The next few years, in respect to our family life, was a mixed bag of segregated experiences—separate trips, separate holidays, and so forth. Our family was required to undergo evaluation after evaluation from more psychologists than I care to report.

For Carrie and I, our response would have been to talk openly with the boys to straighten things out, see to it that their involvement was supervised until they were old enough to understand boundaries, and help them to move on and learn from their choices, not labeling one or the other as victim or perpetrator. But the courts felt differently. Instead, they preferred the route of separation, extensive and ongoing counseling to be sure to keep the event in the forefront of their minds, and to give them each labels. One was labeled "victim," and in session after session, it was made clear to him that this was his humble role. The other was labeled "perpetrator" by the so-called professionals, and he, too, was relentlessly exposed to the label. Carrie-Anne and I were at our wits' end. We despised the labeling and ongoing "treatment," which went on for three years.

For both of us, the experience was a tremendous exercise in patience, forgiveness and release. There were times we both wanted to explode. We felt like we were getting nowhere until each of us finally gave up fighting the battle. We gave in to the process of learning through experience, and things finally began to work themselves out. It was a great challenge, but in the end, our family became more bonded than ever before. In July of 2007, Carrie-Anne and I married in the living room of our home with all of our family and close friends present, including all of our children, victims and perpetrators that they allegedly were.

I learned a great deal about the court system in America through that experience. I came to know all too well the results of our collective egos and the ultimate example of their power: *judgment*. The court system *seems* to be set up under principles of fear, and the responsibilities of the court facilitators *seem* to be designed to judge based on the best story sold to them. In this country, I have come to believe we, as a collective society, find just about everyone guilty until proven innocent. This is a far cry from our original statements of freedom, and a sure sign that our egos are running rampant. Personally, I felt as though I was already guilty in the eyes of the court for not better supervising my children, and without any interest or process assigned to "get to know me and my character," the decision was cast by the judge.

It took me a great deal of energy to work toward forgiving that entire experience. Eventually, though, I released the whole thing and was even able to reunite with my son's mother on a relatively friendly level. To this day, Carrie-Anne works to keep balance between she and her ex-husband, and from time to time, we have to help each other come back to center.

Challenges are there for a reason—to help us grow. Not only are they a life necessity but also unavoidable in a dualistic reality. There just are two sides to every experience, and it must be that way. How else can you experience what you like than to have something to compare to it?

Heaven and Hell

Over time I have mulled over this concept, and through a variety of others' perspectives, I seem to have gravitated toward the notion that, though this reality is incredibly beautiful and awe-inspiring, we may currently be residing in the equivalent to hell. Now, I don't make that statement simply because I've experienced hardship and loss. In fact, I love many things about this reality. I love Nature, people, my dog, beautiful color, the warmth of the sun, the sound of running streams, breezes through the pines, and so much more. Still, I strongly doubt that it is more striking, more profound, more euphoric, or more complete than the pure, unwavering love of the divine source—that which may ultimately be experienced outside of this realty. So, what does that mean? If you view duality as having opposites, what is the opposite of duality (twoness) if not oneness? What is the opposite of a constant struggle for balance if not wholeness? What is the opposite of being inside this reality if not being outside of it? Outside of duality must be where wholeness is truly realized. The source offers pure love, and what is opposite of pure love but *not* pure love?

With the two experiences, one being inside duality and the other being outside duality (which may quite possibly be oneness with God), it seems possible that we reside in a place that offers pain and suffering to learn how to forgive and strive to understand our oneness. I also tend to gravitate toward the idea that we return here time and time again until we finally reach the point when we've released all there is to release through forgiveness. And when that moment comes, we reach a state of enlightenment and return to our wholeness with the divine source.

So, how do we achieve enlightenment? Arguably, this is achieved through the practice of forgiveness and the expression of love. It is the demonstration of love for others, which, in turn, is a love for Self, and the love for Self, which is, in turn, a love for others. It's the extension of respect for those with whom we share this experience, in the same way we wish to be respected. How do we change the world to make it a better place? Through being an example to others and by simply focusing on these same responsibilities in our own lives.

Forgiveness of the Self

Ultimately, the way through a tough situation in our reality is best commandeered with a healthy perspective of yourself within the experience. If we focus on ourselves as individuals, separate from those around us with experiences happening to us, we tend to react from that same vantage point. Typically, the reaction is defensive if the cause is interpreted as an act against us. Our ego-driven perspectives cause us to retaliate out of fear, based on a seemingly realistic moment in linear time. These reactions based on fear feed that fear, giving it more and more power. With each step, the increasing power causes an unconscious but very effective exchange of peace, balance, and mindful thinking for knee-jerk reactions of anger, rage, depression, and so forth. A mind full of negativity leaves little room for any other experience.

The difficult experiences I have had in my life, which I've shared earlier in this book, were not always met with a sound mind and a level head. However, over time, I have learned what it takes to overcome adversity in my life, and the basic premise is actually quite simple. We must simply change our perspective on who we are and who those around us are in the experience. No one is a victim, and no one is a perpetrator. We are all innocent, pure, loving beings outside of this dualistic reality. The actions others and ourselves seemingly commit are simply not our own or anyone else's fault.

The sooner we exchange our current destructive thinking that what is happening is actually happening to us—for the possibility that what is happening is actually just an experience to learn from and can cause us no harm—the sooner we can begin to release ourselves from our belief systems of fear. The exchange lies in becoming an observer of the experience rather than assuming a position within it.

We oftentimes lose sight or simply have never been offered this perspective in our lives, and we therefore see ourselves as a target at a shooting range as opposed to an observer of the actions being carried out.

Some may consider this a dangerous proposition. For instance, if we evaluate the seemingly evil and destructive activities of a serial killer, some may say that what I propose here gives them full license to kill...and this would be true, believe it or not! And to take it one shocking step further, they would be entirely innocent!

However, to bring all of this back into perspective, it must be realized that actions, even though they do not lead to "real" consequences, do lead to an increasing amount of guilt caused by the ego, and this is guilt we ultimately must forgive and release. It also makes sense to point out that the individual who may opt to seemingly hurt another simply does so to themselves. Eventually, they will need to evaluate the experience, forgive it, and then release it to achieve enlightenment. Remember, enlightenment is a return to pure love and wholeness. In the same way, the individual who performs the seemingly alarming action must eventually evaluate, forgive, and release, as will the individual who seemingly experienced the action happening to them. In fact, even those observing the experience must forgive the individuals involved. Why? Because everyone seemingly involved is nothing more than the wholeness and oneness for which you are yourself! We are one, so to forgive another is to forgive Self. One of the most relevant statements of our time is simply: "Do onto others as you would have done unto you." Little else needs to be said, as this statement sums up everything that will help us overcome adversity.

Anything we seemingly do and anything that is seemingly done to us are experiences for which we may choose to forgive or to hold in judgment. It is our choice to make. It is our free will to judge and be judged. Judging another is simply judging ourselves. Causing harm or distress to another is simply causing harm and distress to ourselves. On the other hand, expressing love to another is simply expressing that same powerful emotional energy unto ourselves.

Reading this, you might be contemplating in this moment that following such a practice may open the door to manipulation, and I certainly won't deny that possibility. The seemingly separated selves we experience from day to day are at different stages of the realization of enlightenment. Therefore, there may be those who will take advantage of that position. But forgiveness is the key. Have compassion that they, too, must learn from their own experiences along their path, and that path will eventually lead them home.

I'm not suggesting that we must accept relentless, intolerable actions that are seemingly committed against us. However, forgiveness will eventually bring peace. While we practice forgiveness, we may also make adjustments in our experience to forgo further torment. In my opinion, it is entirely acceptable to establish boundaries while forgiving that individual, or to even release the relationship altogether if it causes distress. However, if we follow this path, we must be sure to release it without judgment. Forgive them, for they are innocent—no different than we are ourselves.

As linear time seemingly passes and the individual reappears in your life, consider allowing them the opportunity to establish a new relationship. Consider the idea that linear time may not exist, and perhaps what we are experiencing is only in this very moment. There is no evidence that our reality existed before or will exist in the future. Approach the opportunity as a possibility for a new relationship—one that will offer a new experience. To deny that opportunity would be to judge based on a past that may never have existed.

In the next few chapters, I will touch more on being an observer, lessons in forgiveness, and our seemingly realistic experience within this reality. I will delve deeper into our seemingly complex reality, and then summarize those complexities into an overall simple concept of expression and projected thought.

Varied Outcomes and the Return of an Old Friend

As I have shared (and as something this book

is largely the result of), my father's passing was the *keystone* moment that led me down a whole new path. In the moment I accepted the telephone call from my older brother that evening back in 1998, I was offered choices to make. Those choices allowed me to develop a perspective of myself in association with that experience. As time went on, that perspective offered new experiences, and with each of them came more choices to make. This cycle advanced my perspective through to each and every character I have typed on these pages thus far.

It could have been very different however. Last fall, I embarked on a quest to find an old friend. She was the mother of one of my high school buddies, and her worldly experiences were some of the first introductions to alternative perspectives on reality that I had ever been introduced to. The family was quite affluent, having been the heir to a large fortune from generations preceding them. The woman had introduced to me the concept of past lives, in particular her relationship with ancient Egypt. At the time I interacted with her, she was immersed in writing a book based on Egypt and had been planning several guided trips there in the years to come.

As time passed, my high school friend and I went our separate ways and lost contact. I always wondered what happened to him, but even with the advent of the Internet, I was unsuccessful in my attempts to locate either of them. In the spring of 2009, however, that all changed.

Having launched a new company a few years prior that was focused on inspiring people to become self-empowered, my thoughts returned to this very special woman. My quest for answers to life's questions had led me to the study of ancient Egypt. The study of so many aspects of modern sciences, ancient symbolism, and alternative views of historical events tends to lead to ancient Egypt. Being that my partners and I had made plans to offer international travel engagements to Egypt in association with research conducted by some of our contributors, I decided to see if I could locate her. In the fall of 2008, I discovered a published author with her same name. I joined the literary group she was a member of and contacted her. As it turned out, the author and she were not the same person. Then, the next spring, I was browsing Facebook and discovered an old friend. We chatted back and forth, and in our conversation, I asked him if he knew what had happened to the family I was seeking. He shared with me that he was Facebook friends with the high school buddy I had been looking for.

I contacted him, and we, too, began to converse. It wasn't long before our conversation turned to his mother and I shared with him that I had been looking to reconnect with them both. He informed me that his mother had died in 1998 of a brain aneurism. Learning this left me stunned and saddened. It was unbelievable to think that not only had she transitioned, but she had done so the same year as my father... and of the same ailment!

We talked back and forth for several weeks and eventually set a date for him to come visit. Only a few months after we reconnected, he was sitting on my couch talking with me face to face. He had driven 2,000 miles to visit, and we were headed on a multi-day backpack trip into the heart of Arizona's Superstition Wilderness.

Sharing that time with him alone was very special for me. As we traversed the trails of the mountain range, we shared stories, philosophical perspectives, hesitations, limitations, goals, dreams, and achievements. Through our conversation I came to understand that he had yet to overcome the loss of his mom. It was certainly understandable to me, considering the very giving and accepting nature of her personality, but I couldn't help but ponder in my own mind as the trail passed below my feet, *What is keeping him from moving beyond the experience? How is it that my father's transition has led me down such a positive path, while his mother's has led him on one more turbulent in nature?*

My first realization was that he and his mother had a very special bond, something that connected them. This was different than the relationship between my father and me. She was a driving force and foundational support system for him, whereas my father and I had not shared a significant part of our lives together. That being said, there still had to be more to the equation. She had passed more than ten years earlier, yet it seemed as though the experience still affected him in a deeply emotional way—so much so that even her wishes to release her ashes in Egypt had not yet been realized.

My thoughts shifted with the inclines and descents of the mountain trail. I didn't want to intrude more than I felt was appropriate, but I couldn't help but consider that maybe his mother and my father had conspired for us to reconnect. It seemed like a clear possibility to me. It wasn't as though I hadn't considered such a concept before. *Could the woman have intercepted my call to find her? Could she have orchestrated our meeting, knowing her son remained trapped by the experience of her passing? Was she aware that I wished to travel to Egypt as she had done so many times in her life? Was she somehow trying to orchestrate a means for her ashes to be spread there, effectively releasing them both?* I knew these were fairly loaded questions, and my assuming that they are a reality might be deemed absurd or even disrespectful to my friend, but in all honesty, the synergy just seemed too real.

As we neared the end of the trail, a remarkable new chapter to the story took place. My friend, who was walking a good pace in front of me, stopped, turned around, and walked back toward me. He bent down and picked up a rock large enough to just fit into his hand. It was an almost perfect pyramid. *What could this mean? Nothing? Or maybe everything?* He placed the rock in his backpack, and we ventured down the trail. As we walked, he shared with me his plan to share the rock with Carrie-Anne. He had met her upon his arrival to Arizona, and we had spent countless hours at our home that first evening in a deep discussion on life. He said he felt compelled to give the pyramid rock to her as a memento. I was amazed by the ongoing synergy and energy flowing throughout this entire experience.

At the end of our adventure, we encountered a man who wandered out of the desert and into our camp. We had camped that evening near my Jeep and were in the process of packing our things when he appeared. He had been lost for two days and had very little water. He was overcome with emotions, elated that he had found someone to help him. He had wandered away from his group, and from what he shared with us, he was more than thirty miles from his car. We provided him water and transportation to his home.

I look back on that experience and wonder if it could have been mere coincidence. Maybe so, but the irony of assisting someone who was at odds in a situation and ultimately returning him home seemed very similar to my experience of finding my friend and possibly helping him and returning his mother home. To some it may seem like a long shot, but to me, having had so many synergistic and symbolic experiences in the past several years, it came as no surprise and actually seemed quite possible.

In any case, he and I reunited, and I now have the answers I was seeking of their whereabouts. I only hope our time together helped my friend in some way to let go of the hurt he was holding so deep within, and allow himself to move forward from that particular experience in his life. He clearly has some amazing gifts to share with the world that he has yet to apply for a greater good.

Better Days Ahead

Without proper clarity and focus, we often find ourselves consumed with fear of the unknown. As we all have been made well-aware, stress leads to health problems, relationship difficulties, depression, and unhappiness. But it doesn't have to be so. There are a number of ways to overcome adversity in life. One of the key methods is to become an observer of life, a concept I've shared previously and will discuss more later in this book. But for now, here are some helpful concepts to consider.

See a lost job as a found opportunity. Don't view it as a loss, but rather as a new beginning. Take a different perspective. Rather than viewing yourself as unemployed, view yourself as *self*-employed. Move away from the idea that you must count on a superior for your livelihood. Consider that you are your own boss—always have been and always will be.

Don't let money make your world go 'round. This is not uncommon at all, and finances are one of the primary causes of relationship disputes. What really matters in your life? The answer to that question is most often not money. Yes, financial security is important to most people, but it certainly doesn't come at the top of the list in most cases. Health, family, love, freedom, and happiness are the things life is really made of. Stop for a moment and find gratefulness for your health. Think about those you love, and appreciate the happiness it gives you.

Healthy healing. Rather than focusing on how your health condition limits you or about a negative outcome that could come from it, focus instead on how you, yourself, can fight back against it—maybe even overcome it. What may have caused it? Consider that it might not be simply a physical reality. Consider that there may be ways to resolve it that don't involve conventional medicine. By all means, get multiple opinions. Take action using a variety of approaches. You may be surprised when you find out what the solution is. Western culture has lost sight of how we, ourselves, can contribute to our own healing. Healing is not about popping pills and going under the knife, though there may be times when this is unavoidable to help resolve the issue. In large part, though, it comes down to our own attitude, intuition, focus, motivation, and beliefs. Healing requires a comprehensive approach.

Guilt feelings. Do you have guilt for something you feel may have adverse effects on yourself or others? Write down your feelings and make a list of possible solutions. Put out positive intentions for a resolution. Then the real work begins! Start by working toward forgiving yourself. In duality, nobody is perfect, and no matter how big or small the issue may appear, it isn't something that can't be overcome. You must realize we are infinite beings of light. We are all innocent. No matter what anyone may say, no matter what label someone may give, you are innocent, and you are loved. It may not seem that way at times, but it is absolutely true.

Believe in yourself. Find clarity in what is important, and move to achieve a resolution with confidence in yourself to be able to do so. Then, find time to get away for a day. It doesn't have to cost much. Take a drive, go on a hike, or enjoy a picnic under a shade tree. Listen to the beautiful birds singing around you, and find peace in Nature's music. Spend quality time with yourself. Then take time with your loved ones. If you are unable to do any of these things, then take a deep breath. Meditate and turn inward, focusing on peace within. Visualize the cool breeze flowing through your hair and the warm sun resting upon your body. With that warmth, allow yourself to clear out energy that isn't serving you.

If there is a will, there is a way. As my dear friend and stepfather always said to me in tough times growing up, "This too will pass. Better days ahead."

Starlight Glow

Warm afternoon and starlight glow as I gaze upon you
I ride on dreams of midnight blue
Wishing away time as the changing eclipse grew

Standing on edge with the glare of Northern Lights
I watch as they dance like glitter in flight
Into the sun's rays, they twinkle bright

As if in slow motion, the particles drift
Resting on rippling waves they shift
Tossing and churning in a fury they sift

Playing tricks on my eyes, I dance with thee
Watching as they swirl and stir around me
Standing upon them, my soul's set free

Caressing the shallows of an ever troubled heart
I sense a new beginning will one day start
Only then will the gentle breeze set in
Creating shivers upon my auburn skin

Focusing again on the changing tide
My expressions of sorrow I must abide
Exposing my softer, more vulnerable side

The sun's rays disappear on horizons low
The time seems to pass on cautiously slow
As the day brings forth once again the starlight glow

~ SC Leuthold

Chapter 4

MOMENTS OF DISCOVERY

The Experiences That Became Life Lessons

Some of the most profound exchanges of knowledge I have ever had in my life resulted from choosing to follow a path of self-empowerment. Having set my sights on expanding my mind through exchanging knowledge with others has had a significant hand in my ever-expanding perspectives.

One of the best opportunities I've given myself has been the formation of a company designed to bring great exposure to new scientific research, alternative healing modalities, and methods for life balance. This project gave me access to incredible minds from all over the world, individuals I would classify as experts in their fields. I have been fortunate enough to entertain extensive conversations with many of these individuals, and through this exchange of dialog, I have discovered how many varying methods and concepts correlate with one another.

Putting a number of methods I've learned into practice has drastically broadened my picture of reality. Keeping an open mind has brought an ever-increasing level of intellectual perspectives to contemplate. The more I seem to allow my mind to grow and expand, the more opportunities seem to present themselves. It is no different than utilizing positive thought for manifesting desires. Like attracts like, and with every opportunity I approach with an open heart and mind, the universe seems to expose me to more and more ideas. At times it is almost surreal.

What I find so exciting about our company, Token Rock, is the idea that such a platform can bring so many different scientific discoveries, theological associations, paradigm-shifting philosophical perspectives, and rediscovered ancient healing modalities together in a context that an individual can use as a grand pallet of colors to paint their own divinely harmonious experience. An opportunity is presented to release them from the gripping control systems and open the door to a new, more balanced and satisfying existence with all things.

It isn't about stepping outside of your comfort zone to visit that distant locale just because you haven't been there before. Rather, the goal is to do so because of what you may discover within yourself by interfacing with the energy that is that place: the smiles on the faces of those who call that place home, the species of life that inhabit the lush or arid landscape, the mysterious and pungent scents that float on the breeze. These things spark new life within.

Pruning your tree of life exposes the limbs and offers an opportunity for the richness of this world to seep in, and from that interaction comes new buds. These buds flourish into healthy new growth, and eventually brightly colored leaves and flowers bloom.

Sometimes, no matter how much we resist allowing the natural process of a forest fire to burn, we must let Nature take its course. From the ashes, new life grows strong and healthy. Some—those who may be particularly close to the experience—may not be able to bare the loss, seeing the cleansing as destruction of what was. Others will embrace the experience as a natural process and eagerly plant their bare feet in the charred, but nutrient soil. In the process, these pioneering souls carry forth the growth of a new and flourishing life.

A Digital Sequence and Consciousness Trigger

One of the early opportunities that presented itself to me was a "prompt," of sorts. A series of numbers began to regularly occur, and I began to see elevens. Seeing numbers regularly is not all that uncommon, but this was different. The phenomenon swiftly swept through my entire family and social circle. It seemed as though each time the experience was shared with someone new, it wasn't long before that individual was seeing elevens too. Our children, our parents, our friends, and everyone we knew seemed to be seeing the same thing.

I was seeing elevens on clocks, on stickers and labels, on license plates, signs, addresses, and advertisements. It was really quite amazing. As my day progressed, it seemed as though every time I looked at the clock, elevens presented themselves: two eleven, three eleven, four eleven, and so on. My own children started pointing out elevens everywhere. What was this odd phenomenon? It didn't take long before we began conducting research on what the meaning might be.

It wasn't all that surprising to discover that the Internet covers "1111" quite comprehensively. We found a number of sites discussing the phenomenon. Through all the information we perused, it became clear that seeing the sequence was somehow related to a spiritual awakening. Some may have their doubts, but for me, this was one of the first moments of realization I had that I was on a particular path—one that would make a real difference in my life if I allowed myself to take it. The 1111 was a prompt; a trigger to launch me into this new adventure of my life. Could it really be that the digital code meant the activation of DNA, a trigger of remembrance and a reactivation of cellular memory? With the binary world of ones and zeros, 1 representing ON and 0 representing OFF, could it be that 1111 represented all systems go? To me, it seemed plausible.

In fact, it became true… to me. Frankly, I couldn't

have cared less what someone else thought of it. To me, it meant something significant. It was a grand moment of personal growth and a confirmation that I was creating a level of consciousness within me that would open the door to something more profound. And in all honesty, it definitely has, simply because the relentless presentation of those numbers led me to conduct a significant amount of research.

When I finally inquired with my friend and colleague, Richard Merrick, author of the book *Interference: A Grand Scientific Musical Theory,* he shared a valuable insight with me:

"It can also be seen in terms of harmonic resonance as it occurs in music or even atoms. It is a fact that the most resonant or energetic interval in music in a major sixth, which is the proportion 5:3. We can express 11:11 as:

*((5/3)*2)^2 = 11.1111111...*

What this is saying is that 11:11 occurs when something is resonating at maximum, then reflected and squared. Now, when space is reflected (as a surface) and squared, it can be said to unfold into a cube. So, 11:11 could be said to represent a 3D mirroring proportion in Nature that creates a highly resonant cube. After all, a string of 1's is an infinity of unity."

It always amazes me how answers lie in deciphering mathematical equations. What Richard may be suggesting here is that the brain resonates in space and may use such a method to connect to the mind and thus, to our higher Self.

The numbers continue to present themselves each and every day of my life, and I continue to believe that seeing them is a continued confirmation of my path. Often when I see elevens on a clock, I try to evaluate what I was thinking about in the moment. Most of the time, it is about a decision that needs to be made, or a desire I wish to have present in my life. In those moments, I at least recognize what I'm thinking about and make a mental note.

Quite often, I even see tens for a period of time, then elevens, and then finally a period of twelves. I tend to believe that seeing tens represents a moment in time preceding something, elevens are the experience transpiring, and twelves represent the resulting experience. I have leaned toward this belief simply based on my own personal observance of seeing these numbers and the experiences I've had when I've seen them. Feel free to come to your own conclusions, but I do encourage you to pay attention and make mental notes. When you do, you may be surprised how often things make sense.

The Miraculous Nature of Numbers

Frankly, other than complex measurements I was

required to calculate back in my twenties when designing electronic toys, I had never been all that intrigued by the nature of numbers. When I began to see elevens, that all seemed to change. I had always been fascinated by the work of visionaries like Albert Einstein, Nikola Tesla, and others, but up until that point in my life, I really hadn't begun to try to understand the significance of their research. I wondered what I had deprived myself from learning and what significance—if any—numbers had in my reality.

Today, I'm regularly amazed by the complexity and simplicity of numbers. Mathematics offers answers to life's questions in ways my mind has difficulty wrapping its arms around, but I make a concerted effort to understand. Like music, mathematics is a universal language. In fact, I tend to view mathematics and music as one in the same. Music is vibration; mathematics is Nature's way to intellectually explain the picture that is painted by that vibration.

Through my ongoing efforts to understand the architecture of this experience by making attempts to understand the significance of numbers, I have been exposed to such concepts as fractals, Fibonacci numbers and spirals, the golden ratio, golden mean, and such insightful tools as numerology, ancient symbolism, astrology, and so much more.

For instance, with numerology I was fortunate enough to befriend two individuals who offered me real perspectives on my own life experience through the use of numbers: Hans Decoz, one of the world's foremost experts on numerology; and the delightful Nancy Laine, our expert numerologist and contributor to Token Rock. On a number of occasions, both of these individuals offered their personal insight to help me better understand my life. Through their expertise, I've learned how my name, my date of birth, my company name, and so many other aspects of my life that are represented by numbers have had a profound effect on my life experience. Now, like anything else, numerology is simply a tool to assist in making life decisions and offers an understanding of why things happen the way they do. It isn't an end-all to the answers we seek, but it certainly does provide some insightful perspectives. In fact, in some ways, numerology has helped me personally with understanding how to effectively communicate with my sons, my life partner, and my business partners. It has given me insights on properly naming my companies, dates for which I should launch those companies for the greatest advantage, and so on. Obtaining numerology reports has certainly been an effective tool for me and for others who have done the same.

An example of how these resources have assisted me can be shown from a numerology report that my wife and I obtained from Nancy in the summer of 2009. It revealed a startling turn of events that was predicted to happen in the coming months surrounding our oldest son. Utilizing the report and a consultation with Nancy, we were able to avoid any seriously adverse effects the events would most certainly have had on him.

Obtaining a report on the person he had been involved with at the time revealed just how incompatible their two life cycles were. By making some adjustments, we effectively removed our son from the situation. Less than a month later, the other individual was in a serious altercation that our son was able to avoid. In a sense, numerology played a very effective role in our decision-making regarding what level of action we needed to take in that situation.

I regularly refer to my numerology report when a new month begins. Just recently, my report revealed that I was entering a five-month cycle, which relates to attraction. My business was in a bit of a downturn, so I utilized this information to attract new projects. I got out, participated in a business social, and walked away with a new client. I observed my experience more closely, aware of the cycle I had entered, and sure enough more often than not, people seemed to come up to me to introduce themselves instead of me having to make the introduction.

These tools may seem esoteric, but that is only because they are stigmatized in the belief systems we were raised under, influencing us away from the truths they may reveal. It is up to each one of us to take a stand for our own existence and explore every tool that is available to find answers and guidance.

New Revelations with Meditation

As I ventured into the realm of purposeful meditation, I began to experience a deeper sense of "me." Being a highly visual person, I had little difficulty getting out of my head and into my deeper mind. These short but peaceful and meaningful moments with myself opened a lot of doors to new possibilities. I was eager to delve deeper and try to make sense of what I had allowed myself to see.

I had been meditating both individually and in small groups. Token Rock had organized a weekly meditation group at the time, so I had given myself plenty of opportunities to explore this new method of getting in touch with myself.

One Sunday evening in the fall of 2007, I had been participating in a group meditation and experienced yet another clear visual series of events that has since remained a fond memory.

I was sitting on a park bench under a tree at the front of what appeared to be an Ivy League college. The building behind me was flanked in old ledge stone. The roof was steeply pitched with stained-glass window details.

As if floating above, I dropped down over the top of myself and took possession of my body. I was wearing a dark suit. I had dark, short hair, and a mustache. Immediately, I stood up and started to walk down the sidewalk in front of me. The sidewalk passed under trees cloaked in a glow of autumn colors. The paved walkway descended down a grassy hillside.

At the bottom of the hill was a stonework footbridge. I walked onto the bridge, making my way down the right side. As I walked across, I saw a woman dressed in a white hat with an oversized brim, adorned with ornate fabric detail. Her white dress was reminiscent of early-day affluence. She was leaning against the side rail, gazing at the stream flowing below. As I approached her, she turned toward me and smiled. I wrapped my arms around her and passionately kissed her. With my hand holding hers, we walked away from the bridge.

The scenes displayed to me one after the next. In the second scene, I was driving an old car—possibly a Model T with its flat, straight windshield and oversized steering wheel in view. Before me was a dirt road with rolling, tall grass hills on either side. I turned my head to the right to see the same woman I had seen before. She was blonde, and this time she was wearing a long-sleeved, white-collared shirt with suspenders. She smiled as I looked at her.

As we made our way down the dirt road, I noticed a white farmhouse on the hill to the right. We turned into the driveway and pulled up to the front of the house, and then the scene changed yet again.

I was now sitting on the front porch of the same house, looking out over the grassy hills. It was a humid day with the comfort of a slight breeze. I sat in a rocking chair. The woman appeared, walking from the front door with a tray on which she carried two glasses of iced tea. She sat beside me. And then the scene changed again.

I was sitting in my bedroom at a desk. It was late evening. I was writing on white sheets of paper by the light of an oil lamp. There was a stack of handwritten papers scattered about. I turned to look behind me and noticed in the dim glow the woman asleep in bed. I got up from my chair and walked toward her and crawled into bed, and again the scene changed.

The final scene of this meditation was the most revealing of all. As the scene opened, the view was from the vantage point of a stage looking out over a crowded auditorium. I walked up to a dark wooden podium before the large audience. They were applauding. As the crowd settled, I said, "I am pleased to introduce my new book, *The Discoveries of Time*, by Orwell Johnston." I turned to my left and spoke again. "I would like to introduce to you the inspiration for my book, Madelline Johnston." The meditation then ended.

Because this meditation was so precise and clear, I began to question its validity. Granted, we do not necessarily validate our dreams, so why would a meditation be any different? I presumed I could attempt to make sense of it. I began researching to try to come to some sort of understanding. Maybe these individuals lived before my time. Maybe Orwell was a past-life experience. My limited research turned up nothing, but the experience wasn't yet over.

A few years later, I found myself lying on a massage table participating in a QuantumPathic® Intuitive Powers Practical Applications course under the direction of my dear friend and colleague, Sherry Anshara. A fellow classmate was utilizing their intuition to discover issues I might be holding onto at the cellular level. As I lay on my back, the individual asked me to close my eyes and take a deep breath. After an exercise to ensure energy was flowing smoothly though my body, the woman asked me to release myself to a deeper level of my consciousness and share with her what I could see.

The scene opened. I again descended down from the canopy of trees and took possession of my body. It was an incredibly bright, beautiful, sunny day. I was at the top of a peaceful, grassy hill. Before me, scattered about on top of this hill, was an ornate collection of carnival rides. Each was brightly painted, precisely detailed, and particularly clean. These rides were clearly new and sat motionless. A bright, reflective glow surrounded each ride, almost as if I could see a thick aura of warm color around each one. I was alone and melancholy. Then I heard the sound of a vehicle passing by. I looked down the hillside and noticed a flatbed Ford, similar to the Model T I had seen in past meditations. It was making its way down the dirt road. In that moment, I realized I had died. I was viewing a place that held deep meaning to me—a place where I had possibly met or shared an experience with someone special.

As the scene changed, I found my view in a spiraling descent to see myself lying on my back in the center of a small wheat field. The field was laid out on the descending hill in front of a farmhouse. I had collapsed. My body was drenched in sweat. The skin on my arms, neck, and face was caked with dust from the wheat harvest. I couldn't breathe. Flies swarmed my face and crawled on my body. The truck I had seen earlier was running idle, not far away. A black man, a friend and fellow worker, was standing over me. I could see the panic in his eyes. He appeared helpless, and he could do little. He picked me up off the ground and carried me to the bed of the truck, and there the story ended.

Lying on the massage table with my fellow classmates in the midst of their own experiences, I sobbed. My story had concluded. I had apparently lived a wonderful life, and in the midst of a hard day's work harvesting my own crop, I met my journey's end. My presumption was that my life with Madelline had come to an abrupt halt. In my transition, I had returned to the hilltop not far from my home, where we had felt a deep connection. The Model T, the farmhouse, the rolling grassy countryside, and the breeze blowing through the giant oak trees took me whirling through an emotional experience that I will never forget.

My classmate conducting the practice proceeded to help me release the experience, forgive it, and arrive at the conclusion that I need not hold on to the pain of that experience any longer. I was deeply touched.

After the exercise, we were asked to share what we had experienced. I told the story to the group, though I had difficulty discussing it without tearing up. I had never experienced a meditation as deeply profound as this, and from it, I shall forever respect the deep, meaningful, and valuable insights that can come from such a practice.

Since that time, I have had many amazing meditation experiences—everything from blue devils to giant flying rabbits distributing golden eggs to children! Some have been quite "out there," and others were very close to my heart. In a few, I even felt as though I were out of body, outside of myself meditating.

I really enjoy and appreciate meditations that somehow introduce the name of an individual. I often wonder if these experiences are replays or alternate realities in which I have participated, like the one I shared previously.

One such meditation I had while participating in another QuantumPathic® course occurred the following year. This particular meditation experience left me feeling a real connection to the natural world. It shed a whole new light on the idea of *Rediscovering Your Divine Music*.

As the scene began, I found myself standing upon the deck of a large ocean vessel. Ominous gray clouds hung low over the surface of the ocean surrounding the boat. The rain had recently subsided. Directly overhead, the clouds broke, and bright sunrays cast their glorious warmth upon us. The air was fresh and crisp.

Before me was a riveted steel staircase. As I raised my head, I noticed a number of individuals standing along the railing, ascending the stairs. As I climbed the steps, I glanced at each one. The first, a woman I did not recognize, smiled at me. The second was my father. The third and fourth were both friends from my early days in college. At the top of the steps, Carrie-Anne stood to welcome me. My dog Xela ("Shayla") sat beside Carrie-Anne, wagging her tail. I was offered a seat in the captain's chair at the helm.

Above my head was a large oval opening in the ceiling. The bright blue sky glowed brilliantly overhead. I closed my eyes; I was floating. Suddenly my surroundings blurred in a high-speed time warp, and in the next moment, everything abruptly stopped, landing me at a beach. The water cast a surreal glow. The sparkle of the waves would have sent a shiver down any observer's spine. A twinkling being of some sort floated before me without words, gestures, or anything. A message was simply felt and became known to me: *"Be the ocean… be the whole ocean."* and I was.

In that moment, I felt the ocean in its entirety. It was an indescribable feeling—a massive wholeness. It was a living, breathing thing that could sense each and every entity it encompassed. It revealed to me a vastness that sensed the slightest touch of a single being entering any shore in every moment, like the caress of a lover lightly touching the surface of the skin with fingertips. It was alive, tender, and complete.

"Be the crab. Feel the minuteness of such a creature among the vast sea. Bury yourself in the cool, damp sand. Feel the satisfaction of that cool comfort against your outer shell. Experience its peace and harmony.

Be the sound of the waves and the whirl of the wind. Know the energy of the curling waves and shifting tides. Know these things. Understand these things. Live as these things, and you will know who you really are."

There was a sudden static… then silence. I was back now on the deck of the boat. The woman I first viewed had now approached me. She said, "I am Melinda Ruth Manchester." I opened my eyes, and the meditation ended.

This meditation meant a great deal to me. I have no idea at this point in my life if I will ever come to know Melinda, but I assure you that I make efforts to know Nature's divine music. The experience this meditation shared with me was one of the most clearly purposeful meditations I have ever had. I gave myself a real life lesson, and this is a lesson I share with you.

We are ALL THINGS. Disbelief of such a concept leads to lack of respect for anything we believe to be outside of us. We simply are not separate individuals. The vibration that makes each of us into form has no beginning and no end. There is a wholeness among what we perceive as separate that is expressed through the analogy of the ocean. The lesson is simple and clear: Be what you see, and ye shall be free. See love, compassion, respect, and gratitude, and ye shall be these things. See greed, guilt, fear, lack of respect for the life of the Earth and its divine creatures, and ye shall know the results of those actions. Our planet is a forgiving mother. She will repeatedly turn a blind eye until her music fades. And, with the faintest tone, she will retreat to heal and will return to triumph again. As if to have overcome a near fatal virus, we will be cast away—not forever, but for now. She will receive us again with open arms to begin anew... giving us yet another chance to get it right.

It is about harmony, about unity, about releasing ourselves from the self-inflicted pain caused by the emotions of lack and fear stemming from individualized greed and selfishness. Find yourself submersed in the divine music, and ye shall find a place among those in complete gratitude.

Words from a Higher Place

There was a time in my life when I might very well have brushed off the idea of possessing intuitive, channeling, clairvoyant, and other "powers." As I have allowed myself to grow and open up to many new possibilities, I have given myself the gifts of knowledge through experience. I am grateful for those experiences, by which I have greatly increased my own intuitive consciousness.

One of the more awe-inspiring experiences I have had is the front-row seat I was granted to watch my own partner, Carrie-Anne, tap into her ability to channel. The perspective we both developed about channeling isn't necessarily what some may project. Carrie-Anne has never delved into questioning why or who she channels. We both discussed it and have tried to come to some sort of reasoning, but that answer just doesn't seem to want to reveal itself. In any case, the messages alone are what we have both marveled at, and the why and who have since taken a back seat.

For me, I think I have simply come to appreciate the profound nature of the words. As far as I am concerned, what she shares comes from something more grand than our human existence, and the messages are revealed to give us inspiration to carry on along this sometimes difficult path we walk.

Her ability to channel launched into existence one afternoon while we were discussing the construction of our website. She had been having trouble sleeping for several nights prior, waking up at the same times each night and then tossing and turning impatiently for hours on end.

After several days, she became more frustrated with her lack of sleep and felt as though there was someone who wanted to express something to her. That morning, she proclaimed aloud her intent to place a pencil and paper next to the bed so she could write whatever it was that needed to be shared.

That afternoon, Carrie-Anne pulled out a sheet of paper to sketch some layouts for our site, but instead of illustrations, words began to flow like a rushing stream. Word after word, page after page, they just poured out from her. After several hours, I picked a few sheets off the floor and began to read them. The words were profound, and they were written in a format that was clearly not her own traditional writing style or terminology. She continued to write for several months, and I read what she shared as the papers piled.

One weekend my son and I decided to go camping in the mountains of Arizona, a fair distance outside of Flagstaff. We had a pop-up camper and set it up along the edge of a meadow. The summertime weather was perfect for enjoying the daytime, but that evening, a storm rolled in. The late night delivered to us a wonderful thunderstorm. The pitter-patter of the rain on the roof brought about a peace within me. My son was fast asleep at the other end of the camper. As I sat under the dim illumination of a glow stick hanging overhead, I picked up my pen light and began reading the thirty pages of channeled writings Carrie-Anne had recently written that I had yet to read.

I recall feeling so deeply connected to her words, and my senses sharpened as I read them. As I turned the pages, the thunder rumbled its deep groan, echoing through the forest surrounding me. As I read, I felt a presence that seemed to encapsulate the entire meadow. It wasn't some strange entity, nor was it a spirit, per se. Rather, I felt the natural environment talking to me. Nature was humming a midnight sonnet with its blowing tall grass of the meadow, the tap dancing of the raindrops, and the rumble of the storm, but there was even more to it than that. It was a real energy connecting me, and the words on the paper were speaking to me, sharing their message of unity and love. I felt small. I visualized my tiny camper among the giant Ponderosa pines. I sensed the vast sea of Nature surrounding me. It was a feeling I will never forget. I was alone, yet I felt a real unity with my world.

Carrie-Anne's channeled writings had been placed before me in black and white, but I felt as though they had been written by me, for me. I began to realize this notion was not so impossible. We are but one, and these words resonated through me no differently than if I had unleashed their power myself. This was a moment of real discovery for me.

As I turned off the flashlight and settled into my bed, I again visualized my tiny shelter among the vastness of this earthly plane. My mind soared straight up into the sky, through the stormy dark clouds, and into the stratosphere to afford myself a view of this magnificent universe, so full of mystery. My mind turned back to see our marvelous blue planet dotted in twinkling lights. The raindrops pattered on like millions of twinkling stars of the night sky as I dozed off into a comforting sleep. I was blessed with this very special experience and will cherish it always.

Carrie-Anne continues to write regularly. Her writings, now known as *Carrie-Anne D'Angelo's Notes From Within ~ The Channeled Journal Writings*, have touched many who have browsed the divine pages. I sense a kinship with those who have read them and have discovered how they speak to them as their own. Life fills us with questions, and Carrie-Anne's words comfort us along our journey to find the answers.

Questions About Our Existence in Physical Form

What is existence? This is one of the more commonly discussed concepts among those I engage in philosophical conversation with. We may believe that through mathematical explanations, our five physical senses, and the seemingly realistic outer world we interact with on a daily basis, that we really are here... but are we? How can we prove we truly exist if we cannot explain where we came from and where we are going? The only explanations we can formulate are those within the laws of the seemingly realistic physics of our reality. Any explanation for this would be outlined within parameters others before us and among us theorized, and these eventually became accepted as humanity's quantitative truth – until, of course, the next theory that seems more likely surfaces and takes hold.

The reality is—or rather, *my* reality is—that I can't prove we are even here in the physical. What if the holographic experience is so refined and complex that we cannot possibly tell the difference? What if we are only *seemingly* here? What if this is nothing more than a projection—like a virtual reality experience—simply put in place to give us a realm we can utilize as a classroom for learning or some other purpose?

I often wonder about this, and honestly, such a concept is what has led me to consider the notion that everyone we seemingly interact with, no matter what judgment we may have placed upon them, is truly innocent. It is also where I have come face to face with fear and have allowed myself to be released from the bulk of it. If we are not truly here, time has no beginning and no end, and our energy exists infinitely, then what can possibly hurt us?

This idea also makes it that much easier to see ourselves in the light of universal oneness. If we are not truly here, then how can we possibly be separate here? This kind of questioning puts me in a bit of a quandary because it suggests that after all of this exploration of self-discovery, I have to accept that I really have no more answers than I did before. But as I choose my seemingly realistic experience, the decisions I make can be based on that concept of oneness, and how I act and react can be a reflection of that fundamental basis.

Raising Children in the Moment of Now

Recently, a question was posed to me about how I was able to raise my children to have good moral values without the structured consequence-driven system of teaching that is characteristic of organized religion. Without the fear of going to Hell or not being accepted into Heaven by a man in a white robe upon their death, how can I possibly teach them to be good upstanding citizens in society? Initially, I had to pause—not because I didn't have an answer, but more so because I had a difficult time comprehending how someone could believe the only way to teach a child is through fear.

Consequently, I proceeded to explain to this individual that teaching children through the concept of a spiritual awakening introduces them to the simplest of universal laws: "Do unto others as you would have them do unto you." This statement, as I have shared earlier in this book, teaches love, fairness, equality, respect, giving, trust, freedom, compassion, and so forth. It really can be that simple.

But what about living in the moment of *now*? How do you introduce to a child the concept of living each and every moment as if it is our last? How do you instill in a child that they need not worry about the future, that they need not hold on to the past if it doesn't serve them, and that, at the same time, they should understand that our choices may have consequential effects we may not prefer in the next moment? How do we teach them the skill of foresight while teaching them not to worry about their next moment of existence?

These are the challenges I have faced while trying to raising my children to be self-empowered, spiritual free-thinkers. On more than one occasion, I have felt the double-edged sword of suggesting my children live in the moment, and then experiencing them not thinking some action through beforehand. So, I have discovered that all I can do is teach by example. I try to live in the moment myself, yet demonstrate how we must still exist within our societal roles. In doing so, we must develop foresight. With foresight, we can do our best to make good decisions in each and every moment. We do not need to live in fear of making the wrong choice, but rather weigh the options and do the best we can, knowing we can make corrections if we must. With each decision we have to make, we should do our best to consider that one universal rule.

Raising a Community of Butterflies—Lessons on Society

A few years after Carrie-Anne and I joined together, we moved into a new home. The wonderful floor plan offered a central courtyard space that had enormous potential. However, upon moving in, we realized the space was nothing but a muddy hole in the ground. It was a blank canvas to create something extraordinary, and that we did. Over the next few years, we created what would become the centerpiece of our home. There is something so rewarding about creating a thing from your imagination with your own bare hands. We created a true sanctuary.

The Butterfly Courtyard was not always known by that name. It only became such a sanctuary when we discovered how attractive the rare passionflower vine, which typically can be found growing throughout the Baja of California, is to butterflies. We had planted and nurtured the vine to an expansive growth that flanked our entire north wall of the courtyard. Often, we would enjoy upwards of fifteen passionflowers blooming at a time. The single-day blooms would quickly fade, allowing new buds the energy to grow.

The butterflies became more and more plentiful with each passing year. At times, we enjoyed sharing the space with sometimes eight to ten fluttering creatures. Each laid their eggs on the passionflower vine and then fluttered away. With this natural progression, we quickly became familiar with the constant balancing act of Nature. The beautiful butterflies, laying their eggs on the vine, offered a succulent place for their offspring to flourish. At first, this was of no consequence to us. We understood the natural progression required that butterflies lay their eggs, and these eggs hatched and grew hungry caterpillars. We enjoyed watching the caterpillars grow, spin cocoons, and eventually emerge, spreading their wings to flutter away. It was an amazing experience to see Nature in action.

That was, until our amazing and hearty passion vines started to become overtaken with caterpillars. There were so many that hardly a leaf survived. The plant was clearly suffering, and unless something was done about it, the plant would die and the butterflies would no longer adorn this beautiful courtyard.

This posed a significant dilemma for us. What could we have done? Or more importantly, what *should* we have done? Would it have been right to intervene? We had planted the vine to begin with, so in a sense, we had offered the vine for Nature's insects to enjoy as much as us, albeit we had no idea at the time of planting that the passion vine was a major attractor of butterflies. The reality became clear that we were being faced with a microcosm of humanity on Earth and the balancing act that must be achieved to sustain the valuable life experience we have been granted.

It was a sad truth. If we failed to manage the caterpillars and eggs, we would fail to save the plant. If we failed to save the plant, the butterflies would no longer come. We loved the plant and its beautiful flowers. We loved the butterflies that made our courtyard their safe haven for reproduction. But it appeared the butterflies had no intention of controlling their own progress or balancing out consumption and production to sustain themselves.

On the brink of complete loss of the vine, we decided to take action. One morning, with buckets in hand, we collected caterpillars and eggs. I transported the creatures to a random bush in a wash not far from our home, leaving them to fend for themselves. For several weeks, we carried out this same exercise until few caterpillars remained. As butterflies laid their eggs, we removed them. When we discovered cocoons, we left them and allowed them to hatch.

Slowly, the plant rebounded and over time returned to its healthy self. Each following year, we allowed the butterflies to flourish until we felt as though the vine could no longer take the relentless harvest of caterpillars. We then systematically removed the caterpillars and eggs for as long as it would take for the plant to return to full health.

Our family learned a valuable lesson about life in balance with Nature. In comparison to butterflies, humans possess conscious thought, and with that ability we are able to make decisions about our sustainability. Butterflies rely on survival of the fittest. The strong—those who are able to withstand the lack of sustainable resources once a plant is extinguished—will survive. The survivors will explore the landscape in search of new host plants. They will do so until no host plants can be found, and only then will they also perish.

How are we any different? Our resources will sustain our human existence until Earth can no longer withstand our relentless destruction. But we are different! We possess conscious thought. We can control our own reproduction. We can control what resources we use in order to sustain our own lives, filled with convenience. We, as a collective mind, can force our societal leaders into the use of energy from the sun or clean fuels, regardless if they feed the enterprising, capitalistic minority. It has to be this way, or like the passion vine, our home will no longer be able to sustain us. This is one of the grand lessons we have been put here to learn, in my opinion. We must learn not only survival, but also to unite and create as much of a balance with our natural world as we can while allowing us to continue to create. What is more important to our survival than unity? What is more rewarding to our existence than sharing the planet with all of the diversity it has spawned? What is more meaningless than the destruction of another species, many of which were here before we arrived?

I'm not proud to have removed caterpillars from the vine. Then again, I must admit that I planted a vine in a place where the vine didn't naturally grow. Maybe where passion vines naturally grow, there are enough of them to sustain the butterflies they host. I live in the desert. The water provided to me that flows from my faucets and shower heads wouldn't be there if it were not for man-made interventions such as dams and canals, and if it were not for those dams and canals, I would likely not live here. I'm no more a solution than I am a problem! But at least I am conscious of this situation and care about it, and that is the first step. We all must become conscious of what we take and give in return. We must remove our complacent thinking and replace it with demanding thinking. As a collective society, we must demand that we force prices down on costly but effective alternatives. We must do so outside of ulterior money-hungry motives, for the greater good of our sustainability.

The mighty sun offers more energy than we could possibly ever hope to produce from any other resource, let alone that of geothermal, wind, wave, and tidal energies. The sun is the answer, the answer to life. This is why so many cultures before our modern society have worshiped its cycles. Without the sun, life on Earth would not exist. It is the foundation of creation and the answer to our most challenging questions of survival. Through it, we will find the balance necessary to continue our legacy here on this very giving and creative planet we call home. In the meantime, though, like the caterpillars, we will continue to be picked away from our existence through man-made diseases and war.

More Lessons from the Passion Vine

As life progressed and the Butterfly Courtyard blossomed into a true sanctuary, I was rewarded once again with its wisdom. The irony of life mimicking Nature always catches me off guard, though it shouldn't. I am an advocate for humanity's reconnection and harmonizing with Nature's divine music. Stopping to listen can be a challenge when trying so hard to focus on societal expectations.

The Butterfly Courtyard has taught me a great lesson about the Earth and our destiny of harmony with it. It is about balance. One morning, I found myself sitting in the courtyard, and it occurred to me that life was once again mimicking Nature. Life had been a mess, frankly, and as I gazed up at the plant, I noticed it had been a while since anyone had removed the caterpillars. Between the hungry creatures and the summertime heat, the plant was looking really beat. I thought to myself and actually acted. I thought that maybe I needed to make more effort to protect the life that was before me if I truly wanted it to survive. Would that be interfering too much in a natural progression? Would it be in my best interest to take action to protect the life I was living?

Then, as I stood there removing caterpillars, my wife appeared and sat behind me, observing. I shared with her my thoughts on the issue, and she offered an interesting response. Not having participated in the removal process of the eating creatures, she said, "It will be interesting to see what happens to the plant." She shared that by not interfering with the relationship between the caterpillars and the plant, one of two things may happen. She stated,"One, the plant will die, or two, the caterpillars will eat all the leaves and have nothing left to eat and the carnage will stop, leaving the intricate stems with nothing but possibility for new life, and again the plant will flourish."

I stood there, still focused on my task, yet very perplexed. Thinking about my own life, I contemplated the fact that I placed high value on the life I was experiencing. I realized I simply wished for it to grow and expand, but for that to happen, I needed to allow the natural progression to take its course—to sit back and enjoy the ride. I considered that as the plant budded new leaves, so would my wonderful life, and with it would come beautiful blooms to share, the *"flowers of life."*

The Great Journey—A Lesson in Monarch Migration

On a more positive note, the influx of butterflies spawned a new interest among my family members in the lives and migration of monarchs in particular.

Recently, we were discussing monarch migration and began to conduct some online research about the amazing journey the butterflies embark on each year. It is a truly amazing journey, to say the least.

For such a tiny creature to be able to navigate its way from as far away as Canada to central Mexico, overcoming such mammoth adversities as numerous expansive metropolises, pollution, weather conditions, and insecticides from crop dusting, let alone having the ability to accurately maintain a bearing on southern Texas for its first major stop and onto the mountains of central Mexico, are almost unbelievable. What I have found additionally remarkable is the volume of these creatures that ascend on these locals each year.

Both Carrie-Anne and I seemed, at the time,

to have a connection to butterflies. One of my favorite quotes of all time was given to the world by the very creative and inspiring writer, Richard Bach, who writes, *"What a caterpillar calls the end of the world, the master calls a butterfly."* These words represent so much in the light of creative thinking and personal transformation.

To me, the butterfly represents so much more than simple beauty. The creature is so delicate and graceful and emits what I believe to be a very peaceful energy. The striking colors and such a wide variety of species make this creature one of the most fascinating in existence. But of all the butterflies, the monarch stands alone as the most awe-inspiring, at least in my opinion.

There are some monarchs that spend their summers in the northwestern United States and Canada that find their winter home in southern California, but for most North American Monarchs, the migration to their winter residence leads them to Central Mexico. Not just anywhere, but to one very specific sixty-square-mile region located in the mountains northwest of Mexico City, near the community of Angangueo, Mexico. No one knows exactly why that location is the preferred winter home to the monarch, but it is. The monarch's unique winter habitat has been discovered at only twelve regions on the planet, and the monarch's story is one of Nature's most incredible examples of adaptation and survival.

What makes this journey so incredible to me is

not only the ability the monarchs have to stay on course for such a distance to reach particular locales in Texas and then on to Mexico (approximately 2,500 total miles), but the fact that upon their return north in spring, the creatures pass along their legacy to four consecutive generations before returning back in the fall. You see, when spring arrives, the monarchs awaken from hybernation and depart from their winter home in central Mexico and head back toward southern Texas to mate. Here, the monarchs lay their eggs on milkweed plants for the next generation of butterflies to carry on the journey. After laying their eggs, the monarchs flutter around for a few weeks and then die. Having flown from as far as Canada to Mexico the previous fall, winter hibernating in Mexico, and then flying their way back to Texas in spring, this generation of creatures finally meet their journey's end. (Note that there are some unconfirmed routes that may not pass through Texas, but it is primarily believed that the butterflies travel through that state.)

When the eggs hatch (typically in May or June) and the caterpillars mature, form their cocoons, and incubate long enough, they emerge, spread their wings, and flutter away as the second generation of the year. This second generation continues north, laying their eggs along the way. This second generation only survives for a few weeks beyond laying their eggs, and then they too transition, passing on the legacy to the third generation. This new generation (hatching typically in July through August) carries on the process before meeting their fate only about six weeks later. In September and October, the fourth generation is born. No one knows quite why, but this generation is different from the others. The new offspring, the third decendents of the original monarchs of the year, somehow know what journey lies before them, where they must fly, and how to get there. This generation begins a long journey that eventually leads them to Mexico. And, unlike the generations before them, these descendants survive for six to eight months in hibernation on the trees of their winter home. Thus, the process begins anew the following spring. To me, the story of the monarch is amazing and inspiring beyond most tales of distant journeys.

A group of researchers who study monarchs conducted a test wherein several of the butterflies were tagged with tracking devices. The creatures were specifically selected from the Midwest and relocated to the eastern seaboard, tagged, and released. The researchers wanted to see if the creatures could still find their way to Texas and on to Mexico. As the monarchs departed, they flew directly south toward Florida. Considering the fact that these creatures would find themselves flying over the Gulf of Mexico, with no place to land, they would likely not make it to their winter home. However, astonishingly, as the creatures reached the deep South they turned west, correcting their bearing, and headed directly toward Texas, eventually reaching their destination.

What does this say about our world? What does

this say about our own species? What potential do we have to overcome adversity? What laws of Nature gauge and guide us on our journey that we have yet to discover?

If such a tiny, delicate creature can make such a monumental journey in life while overcoming such enormous odds, what say you about your own life?

If such a remarkable legacy can bring us together the way the story of the monarch does, what say you about your legacy?

If such a species that spreads its population to such exponential distances apart can come together as one united population each and every year to carry on the success of its own kind, what say you about the unity of the human race?

Consider the concept of *fractals* (as described in the Token Rock Subject Library): "A fractal is a rough or fragmented geometrical figure in which an identical motif is repeated on a reducing scale. The pattern is whole and complete unto itself, but if you take any little portion of this whole out and examine it closely, you'd see the pattern repeating itself again and again infinitely. This fractal is called a Mandelbrot set, coined by Benoit Mandelbrot in 1975. This fractal geometry is closely associated with chaos theory. It represents a mathematical point where chaos and order merge."

I find that we, as humans, can learn a great deal from the study of infinitely larger and infinitely smaller components of our existence. And looking at the monarch butterfly tells me a great deal about what we, as humans, are capable of achieving.

You see, we can overcome great odds to achieve great things. We can also step back and take a good hard look at our actions and make corrections for the betterment of our existence. We can be humble and proud at the same time. We can make room for the small sprout to grow among the great giants in the forest. We can build the tunnel, and we can create the light at the end of it to lead our fellow man, our future generations to make their way. It can be done. It will be done. And we shall be magnificent.

Sharing Knowledge in Belize

Since I had begun walking my new path after that profound day on top of the mountain years earlier, I managed to spend some of my time traveling to some of the more remote parts of the world. When Carrie-Anne and I entered a relationship, she was also longing for world travel experiences.

Our first trip together was a return trip for me to the Central American country of Belize. Until the late 1970's, Belize was under the control of Great Britian and mapped as the colony of British Honduras. When the country gained its independence it was re-named. As the country developed, it opened up to the world as a tourist destination, but even today, most of the country is pretty quiet to tourists. Only the northern coastal island town of San Pedro on Ambergris Caye and the coastal community of, Belize City, are very populated.

We had an extraordinary time on our travel to the country, but one particular moment stands out even today as one of the more memorable experiences of that time, an experience I will never forget. It is a moment of time that sums up a great deal about the real value of world travel.

After landing in the Belize City airport, we traveled by taxi to the boat docks along the coast. Here, travelers can purchase tickets to board speedboat taxis that offer nonstop express travel on the turquoise waters of the Caribbean to a variety of barrier reef islands. On our ride to the island of Caye Caulker, a backpacker's island located about ten miles off the mainland, we encountered three individuals sitting across from us. We began talking with them and discovered that they, too, were from Arizona. Two were dating, and the third was the girl's brother. They had recently joined up somewhere along shores of the Yucatan Peninsula following individual travels and were headed to the island for a few days of relaxation. Our friendly conversation grew into a dinner date, and that evening, Carrie-Anne and I joined our new friends at a quaint Italian restaurant. The place was quiet, being that we were visiting in the off-season. Following dinner, we found a wonderful place to sit and chat at the end of a long dock suspended over the dark evening waters of the sea. The stars were twinkling so brightly it felt as though we could select one and put it in our pocket if we'd dared. The cool breeze delivered the salty scent from the exposed corals of the distant barrier reef and beyond. As the waves lapped against the posts of the dock, we engaged in conversation about the world, life, religion, social interaction, and philosophy until the early hours of the morning. The conversation left me with such a positive experience. I found myself greatly appreciating not only the opportunity to meet and connect so deeply with these individuals, but also for having had the experience at the end of a long dock off of a tiny island in the middle of a vast ocean. It seemed like we were the only people on the planet, and nothing else mattered but the moments we were sharing.

I can't help but look back with sentiment on that experience and many others like it that I have had with new friends. I find that the more I open up myself to being known and knowing others, the more I connect with who I truly am. These fine individuals have given me insight and inspiration along my own life path, and I presume I have done the same for many of them. In reality, though, these individuals were opportunities I gave myself to learn and grow, and for a moment in time, we were able to connect in a way that allowed us to experience a step toward the oneness we have all forgotten.

Experiences like these are what lead me to believe that the more open we are, the more social and responsive we are to meeting new people and sharing new ideas, the more we are able to inwardly grow and outwardly express.

Compassion for the Rabbit – Another Life Lesson

A profound life lesson played out before me one morning. Since I was open to embracing it, I've since given myself the opportunity to harvest many profound revelations about this reality in which I've found myself in.

My life had been full of trauma drama as of late, and I had allowed that drama to guide my life for several weeks. I had been pushed into a difficult experience kicking and screaming and had tried relentlessly to claw my way out of this vacuum hole, to no avail. Nothing seemed to sway the experience in the direction I apparently desired. "Why?" I asked. "Why is this happening? I clearly didn't ask for it. I clearly don't desire it."

I allowed the experience to affect me so deeply that I lost more than ten pounds off of my already lean body—weight loss that didn't really serve me well. Through this process, I had wholeheartedly attempted to apply every technique I had learned and shared with others. Sometimes one technique will work in a situation, while another one will work better in a different situation. This time, what proved to be effective was a visit with my friend Serica, an acupuncture practitioner. She spent two sessions working on my lower stomach, where I was clearly holding all the pain and suffering I had projected onto myself.

As she applied the needles, I almost immediately began to cry. I couldn't stop it; the tears just came. After leaving her facility and returning home, I allowed all the emotional turmoil to release from my body. I sobbed harder than I had when my father died. Yes, it was sadness, but it was much more than that. It was me, allowing it to affect me and not releasing it to the universe.

As I worked to resolve the situation, one that may not have appeared at first glance as favorable, I really gave myself an opportunity. Everything was going to be okay. I came to realize this because of the profound experience I had one summer morning in the midst of the drama.

I decided to take my family to California for a few days. Our Arizona home had become something of an island. The 114-degree heat had kept us inside, cooped up with little breathing room. We had extreme cabin fever. The drive to California was horrendous. The kids were constantly bickering. Though we had the air conditioning on, the heat outside remained over 100 degrees until only about a half hour before we reached our destination in Fallbrook. Upon arrival, we were greeted with sixty-degree temperatures and some welcoming light humidity.

The next morning, as the sun rose over the rolling hills surrounding my sister-in-law's home, I decided to get up and take a walk by myself. I bundled up and headed down the road. I soon discovered a horse path and followed it for about a mile through the rolling hills and thick tree-lined valleys. Eventually the trail ended at a country highway. I headed down the highway en route back to the main road to the neighborhood where I was staying. Cars buzzed by every few minutes. The highway was narrow and winding with only a narrow shoulder. I walked on, deep in thought about my life. Then, about fifty yards in front of me, the next act of my life took place. God, the universe, the source—whatever you feel comfortable calling it—delivered to me a life lesson.

As a large SUV rounded the corner ahead of me, I watched as two rabbits entered the highway; only one made it to the other side. The second rabbit ran across, and as it made its way toward the other side, it second-guessed and turned back, and it was struck by the vehicle. Still a distance in front of me, I walked toward it. Cars continued to buzz by, swerving to miss the casualty (probably in an effort to avoid getting blood on their paint job rather than for any benefit of the creature). As I approached, I noticed the creature was still alive. It lifted its head repeatedly, attempting to get up. It was clearly in shock. I stopped on the side of the road as cars continued to buzz over the top of it. When the road cleared, I walked out, picked it up, moved it to the side, and sat down on the side of the road beside it. It watched me intently. Its heart was pounding, and its left eye was bleeding. Other than lifting its head, the rabbit couldn't move. I began to talk to it, to pet its back and ears, encouraging it to live.

I'm not really a tree hugger, not a Buddhist, no vegetarian, and not a member of PETA. I'm not against hunting for food in order to survive. My perspective on life is simple. We ARE all one. We ARE connected energetically to all things. We MUST, as a species, reconnect with the divine music of Nature. I connected with this creature not just for the creature, but for me. My encouragement and compassion for the rabbit, I am certain, transcended the connection between us. It projected out on a grand scale and to every particle of this reality like a holographic image.

I proceeded to conduct healing energy techniques I had learned on the rabbit and sat with it for almost an hour. Cars were still buzzing by no more than three feet in front of the two of us, but I felt if the rabbit was there for a reason, so must I be.

As time went on, the rabbit more regularly lifted its head. I eventually adjusted its position to encourage it to get up and move around. Then, as I stood up, it did as well and began to hop around. Likely in a daze, the rabbit began to hop back onto the highway, so I moved it far off the road into the tall grass. Within about fifteen minutes, the rabbit was hopping around. I shared with it that it could live—that I wanted it to live, but that I wouldn't take it home with me to care more for it. I wanted it to be wild and return to its partner.

I learned such a profound lesson from this

experience. It may sound cliché, but when the world beats you down and you are lying on the pavement with blood pouring out of your body, you must, MUST lift your head off the highway and survive. If someone is there to help you, let them. They love you enough to care, and that love is what will heal your wounds. Life WILL be OKAY. You WILL survive... and not just survive, but live happily again. At the time, it was so hard to see it that way through all of the belief systems I'd allowed into my life, but I believed in that moment that I would be okay.

As I walked away down the highway, I was so grateful for the experience I had with that rabbit. I walked with my head high. I couldn't help but wonder if those passengers in the cars coming at me, buzzing by at fifty miles per hour, could read the shirt I was wearing: "Carpe Diem (Seize the Day)." That was exactly what I did. It was a day of the solar eclipse, a new day. A warm aspect was there to share its love, and I was surrounded by it.

As I wrote about the experience, I sat at the kitchen table sipping hot tea. The tea tag read a meaningful quote of the day: "When you know that all is light, you are enlightened." Everything IS light. Everything is energy and interconnected. That rabbit was part of my experience in this world, and I am grateful it was there for me to connect with it.

Song [Secret Love]

I hid my love when young while I
Couldn't bear the buzzing of a fly
I hid my love to my despite
'Til I could not bear to look at light
I dare not gaze upon her face
But left her memory in each place
Where ere I saw a wildflower lie
I kissed and bade my love goodbye

I met her in the greenest dells
Where dewdrops pearl the wood bluebells
The lost breeze kissed her bright blue eye
The bee kissed and went singing by
A sunbeam found a passage there
A gold chain round her neck so fair
As secret as the wild bee's song
She lay there all the summer long

I hid my love in field and town
'Til e'en the breeze would knock me down
The bees seemed singing ballads l'er
The fly's buzz turned a lion's roar
And even silence found a tongue
To haunt me all the summer long
The riddle nature could not prove
Was nothing else but secret love

~ **John Clare**, 1920

Chapter 5

RECONNECTING WITH SELF

Taking the First Steps

I have been asked from time to time what led me down the path of spiritual awakening. In trying to answer this question, I found myself writing a description (shared earlier) of what I feel an awakening process is. The truth is, any explanation I may provide in this book is simply my own. I tend to believe that, all being on our own path, we each find our spirituality at different ages and stages of our experience.

For me, though, I sat down one evening and really attempted to outline the historical chronology of what led me to put spirituality in the foreground of my life.

1. Why Would God Be Judgmental?

I grew up Catholic. Funny how making that statement so often returns the response, "Say no more." Yes, I was baptized and eventually took communion and spent every Sunday in catechism. I didn't have a choice. My parents were Catholic, so I was led into the program. Eventually, after my mother and father divorced when I was in fourth grade, my mother remarried and became Lutheran and then Congregationalist. Because she was my primary caregiver, I became a Congregationalist too. Frankly, I have no idea what the difference is between the three organizations other than the fact that priests can't marry. What I do know is that they all follow the Bible, take communion, and meet on Sundays in a church, and each of the three leaders were dysfunctional just like me. None of them had the answers, none of them truly happy that I could tell, and none of them convincing enough to give me reason enough to halt my search for my truth.

As I moved out of my childhood and into my adulthood, I became disgusted by the whole concept of religion. For quite some time in my life, just hearing the words "God," "Jesus," and "Bible" made me cringe. My spirituality has offered me a new perspective, though, and with it, I have been able to see why I felt that way.

My real questioning (once I got over the terminology and separated myself from organized religion) became more about what the religious leaders had told me was my reality. I, like all religious followers, had been led to believe that God is planning to judge me upon my death—and although He loves me, He will sentence me to eternal hell if I don't believe in Him before I die.

I couldn't understand why God would be such an unforgiving, judgmental being when He is the alleged creator of the whole thing. Why would He create war, hatred, pain, and suffering? Why would He have any trait that would reflect ego if He is supposed to represent true unconditional love? Is it designed to test us, or are we led astray by power hungry leaders who only wish to control us?

2. What Is Reality?

Around the same time, typical questions began to surface more regularly within me about my reality. I wanted to know who I really am, why I am here, how I got here, what my purpose is, and so forth—basically the same questions we all have. Though I have my opinions about these questions, I remain open to new ideas and have yet to give myself all the answers. Nevertheless, I am certainly more content following a path of self-discovery to find my own answers than to simply accept a routine response.

3. Where Would I Find the Answers?

One of the more profound realizations I had in

the process was to discover that nobody has the answers but me. I put myself here for a reason, and the quest to find the answers to life brought about lessons to learn from. And in these lessons I would find the answers I seek—my own answers.

4. Techniques to Make a Connection.

I began researching and practicing techniques to connect with my Self. This was a big step in the process, one I continue today. Once I finally began to utilize techniques such as meditation, tapping into my intuition, and conversing with my higher Self, I began to formulate a position about who I am, why I am here, how I got here, and so forth.

Much of the trouble, I discovered, is that we consume ourselves with noise and distraction. Clearing the mind and opening the heart allowed me to get beyond the limitations that occupy my existence.

5. Oneness Prevails.

As I practiced peaceful living, being an observer, and delved deeper into research on so many different subjects, my beliefs began to shift from a separation between me, my fellow Earthly inhabitants, and God, toward an attitude of oneness with all things in my reality.

6. The Discovery of Spirituality.

With the concept of oneness as my foundation, I began to sense a kinship between my Self and Nature. I began to see that there was no separation between my surroundings and me. Nature and I (God) were one, and being so, our energy was universal. This I called spirit, and for me, this connection became my spirituality.

7. Lack of Evidence that We Exist.

As I practiced my spirituality, I began to encounter a few road blocks. I eventually had to come to terms with the realization that there simply is no proof, no evidence that anything exists now, existed before, or will exist in the next moment. All there appears to be is this moment.

I took hold of this concept and began to see how important it is to let go of what isn't serving me in my life, and to ask for more of what I truly want in my life. In the process, I began to have the life lessons I feel have opened my mind and heart and have allowed me new strength and wisdom.

8. Self Is the Subconscious Mind.

Without any ability to prove my physical existence, I came to realize that Self simply is not physical. Self is the subconscious mind, and this is something I cannot touch that resides somewhere else outside of this seemingly physical reality.

9. My Higher Self Resides Outside the Physical.

I contemplated that since Self acts as the subconscious mind, and that the mind is outside of the physical realm, my 'higher self' (my essence or spirit—my connection to the source) must reside outside of the physical.

10. God is My Higher Self

By contemplating the reality about my Self, I came to the conclusion that my higher Self, being my essence and spirit, is God. I acknowledged the perspective that being so, God must reside outside the seemingly physical realm.

11. Physical Is an Illusion.

With the perspective that my Self, being God, resided outside of the seemingly physical realm, I came to perceive the physical simply as an illusion. The energy and vibration that shapes us into a physical existence must simply be projected thought.

12. Reality Is an Illusion.

I considered that if the physical is an illusion and is simply a projection, then the purpose of this experience, the projection, must therefore be something of significance to us from outside this reality. Could it possibly be a place for learning? If so, then to learn what?

13. Meeting the Ego.

I took a good hard look around this projection and began to notice just how powerful the ego is. I started to see how this could be a learning experience. Maybe we are projecting a dualistic experience, one that is certainly difficult—if not impossible—to truly balance in order to release the egocentric ways. To release greed, hate, anger, frustration, lack, disease, discontentment, pain, and suffering... all for the unconditional love of all things, that which is God.

14. Forgive and Release.

As I began to make attempts to release the ways of my ego, I was pleasantly gifted with the process of forgiveness. Through a lot of thinking and ongoing practice, I have since come to find that forgiveness starts with the Self. As I've begun to see others as part of the whole (the oneness known as God or the source or what have you), I have found that by forgiving myself and releasing the experiences that have held me down, I have had a much easier time doing the same for all experiences in life; including the experiences that involved other seemingly physical beings, my fellow mankind.

If I can view the world as an illusion that I have created, then I can see all things in that illusion as being part of me. If I can master forgiveness of my Self in this illusion, then I release the ego, and judgment with it. Upon my death, judgment would not exist. I, being one with God, would not possess judgment. Without darkness, we are left with pure light. Without ego traits, we are left with pure, unconditional love.

15. Releasing Our Bond to this Physical Reality.

Through the process of forgiveness and release, I began to see a means for releasing what bonds us to this physical reality cycle, and ultimately returns us to our true oneness—oneness with our higher Self, which is God.

16. A True Effort Toward Forgiveness and Release.

This phase is one I have yet to fully exercise. It is the ultimate sacrifice in this reality to forgive and release as a primary action in life. With this forgiveness comes peace and unity in this reality. I ponder if it can be so in duality. Possibly not! I often wonder, if we all practice true forgiveness and release as our primary action, would we eventually completely release the ego? If so, I wonder, too, if this reality will cease to exist—not from destruction, hate, and differences, but from complete unity, which could negate the purpose for the projection.

The difficult part of this is my own limitation that I'm not so willing to let go of. Honestly, I enjoy being here and experiencing all that this experience has to offer, even if it is an illusion. I feel as though I can work on practicing forgiveness and release, and yet enjoy this experience to the fullest. I can be in awe as to the amazing and intricate illusion I have created and work toward truly loving all that is within it—me.

I ponder if we may discover that the sacrifice of acting wholeheartedly and decisively on forgiveness and release was never a sacrifice at all.

Wrinkled Mind

Blindly wandering, wasting time
Willfully motionless without rhyme.

I seek to understand the mysterious reason
Inspiration adjourns with each changing season.

Into the hallowed halls of steel
There must be triggers, though strangely surreal.

Alone in the world, these tempests creep
Into the caverns of darkness and deep.

How is it they can survive?
They wish nor want to be alive.

Stirring our thoughts and fears
These troubles command us like daggered spears.

Look no further than the wrinkled mind,
And be open and aware of what you may find.

It is here these things lay
Collecting dust day after day.

And in a startling quiver
They strangely appear in the rush of a shiver.

When this day comes, do not pretend,
Or expect an uneventful end.

For those who look them face to face
Will learn the mysteries of time and space.

~ SC Leuthold

Chapter 6

TOOLS FOR THE TASK AT HAND

Putting What We Know Into Practice

There are many very effective tools that can help one with self-empowerment and spiritual growth. Along my own path, I have met a great number of people who have offered their insights on what has worked for them, and I have utilized much of this advice with wonderful results. With a little effort, you can also begin to lift the heavy weights you have placed upon your own shoulders. Let's take a look at a few of these tools.

Positive Thinking and Manifestation

Today the term "manifestation" is becoming popularized through various published books and films, most of which are designed to introduce readers and viewers to such manifestation principles as the "Law of Attraction."

Manifestation, or "to manifest" something, is to bring about in the physical world that which we desire. The seeds of manifestation are thoughts, feelings, and emotions. Manifestation is the process of cause and effect and the utilization of these expressive variables. This process effectively materializes a result based on the cause.

Our thoughts, feelings, and emotions are the tools we use to manifest, or to bring forth, experiences in our reality. Our entire life is nothing more than a series of experiences comprised of manifested possibilities we have incorporated into our lives. In life, we are free to make choices in each and every moment. These choices are based on possibilities that present themselves to us based on what we attract utilizing these tools. This said, we can conclude that what we think and feel, how we react to those thoughts and feelings, and what we communicate through words and body language greatly affect what we attract to ourselves moment-by-moment.

There are a variety of methods that have surfaced over time that help individuals master manifestation, using it as a tool to realize what is desired. Ultimately, however, it comes down to attitude, self-esteem, and a better understanding of who we are as individuals at the deepest level. It is about being able to look at ourselves with real eyes and having the courage to face our fears, release our self-instilled limitations, and utilize our intuition to better understand why we think, feel and react to those thoughts the way we do.

As was stated earlier, it is widely accepted in the scientific community that our thoughts, feelings, and emotions emit vibrational frequencies. If true, wouldn't it also be reasonable to assume that the vibration we emit will resonate with other like vibrations? If what we emit is what we resonate with, wouldn't a more satisfying result be to emit thoughts, feelings, and emotions that will resonate with what we truly wish for in our lives rather than what we do not? This is the basis for the Law of Attraction and the movement toward self-empowerment.

If what we feel is depression, sadness, lack of something in our lives, loathing, anger, guilt, or other destructive behaviors, then what our physical selves will experience is destruction. If how we react to experiences is with excessive stress, we can only expect our bodies to manifest results caused by stress, including continued stressful situations and, ultimately, disease.

If instead what we feel is happiness, excitement, love, satisfaction, appreciation, and other positive behaviors and emotions, then we will attract the same. It is simply our own choice to decide how to feel and how to react to what seems to happen to us.

In his book *Hidden Messages in Water*, scientific researcher Dr. Masaru Emoto demonstrates the affects varying vibrations generated by words, sounds, and music may have on water crystals. As well, recall my earlier discussion that thoughts, feelings, and emotions generate vibration. It could be concluded that these three expressive variables have an effect on our own physical cellular structure, just like with the water crystals. And, if the vibration can affect cellular structure, couldn't it also have an effect on the frequencies our existence attempts to harmonize with outside of our physical bodies? Like attracts like. If everything in our reality is interconnected as one collective energy, why can't our own existence have an effect on reality as a whole? It not only can... it DOES!

No differently than how a change to one small part of a hologram affects the entire holographic image, changing our thoughts, feelings, and emotions changes the big picture as well. We effectively paint a portrait of ourselves through these three mediums, and this portrait is projected to our entire reality, where our reality acknowledges that vision of ourselves.

Manifestation has a direct effect on our physical health, our relationships, our finances, our daily experiences, and so on. Mastering manifestation as an effective tool opens the door to realizing your dreams. It gives us the tools necessary to make positive changes in our lives, to a reality that serves us more effectively and more productively. But, it does require effort.

So, how do we actually begin to change the way we have been programmed to think, feel, and react? This begins with first opening our minds to the possibility that altering these variables can actually work. The next step is to begin being completely honest with ourselves, no matter how hard this may be to face. Start to seriously assess your thought process, how you truly feel physically and emotionally, and how you react to difficult situations in your life.

What many have not yet grasped in regards to this concept is the depth at which our thoughts, feelings, and emotions are entrenched. These three components are developed early on in our childhoods, based on influences that shape our perspectives during those impressionable years. These perspectives are born from varying positive and negative feedback we have received, limitations we have placed on ourselves based on self-esteem or lack of self-confidence and the like. Until we face these issues, we may not be able to fully express what we desire and remain on that positive path to achieve our goals.

A desire to understand how our childhood experiences have had such a profound influence on who we are today and how we can break the emotional habits we have developed is often what inspires many people to seek specialized personal growth workshops.

Becoming the Observer

As I've mentioned in other parts of this book, I am a strong proponent of the practice of being an observer of your own life. I participated in a series of workshops several years ago that really helped put my life into perspective. The courses taught a great deal about tapping into my own intuitive powers to help facilitate healing my own body. Then, once that concept was clear, the course introduced the practice of becoming the observer of my life.

By becoming observers, we allow ourselves to realize that what may be happening is only happening *around* us and not to us. Putting this realization into practice gives me the tools I need to avoid being manipulated by any situation that is designed to create fear and may lead to guilt, sadness, the feeling of lack, and so on. Though it isn't always easy to remain the observer of a situation, it certainly is an effective tool for avoiding feeling victimized. Observing your life in action like you would while watching a movie or play allows you to really see what each character in the scene may or may not be doing. It gives you the advantage of making conscious choices based on observing the experience rather than orchestrating a reactionary response based on offense or defense. Doing so also creates a very interesting experience. I always seem to be excited about what is going to happen next.

Additionally, as an observer, we have the ability to look at our physical bodies and utilize our intuition to assess what physically and chronically ails us. Then, with additional tools available, we may work toward resolving those ailments through a process of release.

Consciously Creating Your Experience

There was a moment in my life when I really started to understand the whole concept of being a conscious creator. The experience was quite meaningful to me at the time. I wrote about it in my journal and eventually shared it as an article. In any case, it speaks a great deal about how I finally started to achieve higher levels of conscious creation. I admit I also believe that in duality, mastering such a concept is nearly impossible, simply because of the variables of cause and effect and duality's purposeful imbalance. Yet, I also believe it is a worthy time investment to practice such a concept.

Analogy of a Shadow ~ Understanding and Being the Creator of Your Experience

My eyes were closed, covered with the palm of my hands, elbows resting on my knees. As I opened my eyes, my view was of the floor before me. The light shining from the bulb on the ceiling cast a shadow on the floor that startled me. It was of my head, but because my hands, which had been over my eyes, were now resting against the sides of my head, my fingertips appeared like the horns of a devil, and my protruding thumbs looked like the devil's ears. *How silly*, I thought.

As I moved my hands around the sides of my head, the shape changed again and again. Different figures appeared before my eyes as the different positions of my hands took shape. The voice in my head spoke.

Like a shadow, we each take different shapes. A shadow cast from the same object can take very different shapes, depending on the changing of the laws that govern that shadow. When the sun is high in the sky, the shadow will be short and fat. When the sun is setting, the shadow will be very long and narrow. Like a shadow, each of us is cast in the same likeness, but each infinite one of us may (and does) take a slightly different shape.

As my eyes moved around the floor, I noticed a weight scale in the corner. The scale was white with silver circles where the balls of your feet would be positioned, and smaller silver circles where the heels would be positioned. They were offset with the larger ball circles pushed out toward the edge of the scale and the heel circles inward, closer to the middle. Down the center, between the feet position, were two buttons stacked one above the next. The shapes, though obvious of their purpose, together formed one unified shape that one would not recognize if the parts of the whole were separate. Together, however, the shapes formed a surprising pattern of a butterfly.

My thoughts directed me to consider that the parts of a whole may not necessarily be recognizable unless the whole is considered a shape in itself.

As I walked around my master bathroom, I began to contemplate wealth. I came to realize that the only way to experience wealth is to experience the opposite. As Neal Donald Walsh shares in his novel, *Conversations With God* (my interpretation of his writings), an experience of something can only be experienced if you have the opposite to compare it to. This isn't to say that to experience wealth you must first experience poverty. It simply means that to experience wealth, or to appreciate the experience of wealth, you must first be able to understand how it feels to not be wealthy. In this state, you can understand the true nature of the experience of wealth. To experience "with," you must, at some point, experience "without." These occurrences may be in the same life plane or over more than one.

As I turned on the shower and felt the water, I discovered the water to be cold. Quickly, I turned the dial to a hotter temperature. As I did, I felt the water and adjusted the temperature to one that suited my level of comfort. My thoughts turned to such a simple analogy—that of the water temperature I was now experiencing. In order for me to find the temperature that comforted me appropriately in the moment, I had to first experience the water at a temperature that didn't suit me. Thus, cold water and hot water were experienced. I then adjusted the dial until the temperature reached that which I found to be the most suitable.

Life can be very much summed up in a similar fashion. In order to experience what life has to offer and to find the place in this world that suits each of us with the satisfaction we all seek, we must experience what the world around us has to offer. We test out different experiences and find those that suit us. We first must feel the cold and hot temperature of the water before we can find the temperature that satisfies us.

This isn't to say that we must experience the extremes of each. We are intelligent beings. As infants, we quickly learn the extremes of the experiences we have. We quickly learn that we do not appreciate extremely cold or hot water. Therefore, as older beings, we already understand that the dial on the shower offers the experience of the extreme opposite temperatures. So as we turn on the faucet, we immediately and more efficiently move the temperature to a position that is likely to be closer to that which we will find satisfaction.

So, to experience extreme wealth, you need not experience extreme poverty. You can if you wish, and to do so would likely result in a richer experience of what life has to offer, but it isn't necessary. At one time or another in one's life, we may have experienced what it is like to be short on cash, while at another time in life, we may have experienced what it is like to have a little extra cash available to us. These experiences can sum up for us the opposites of the two enough for us to get a taste of what it is like in either situation. Therefore we can choose to follow a path that suits us more effectively. If it is more satisfying to one to experience the latter, then the dial on the faucet can more effectively be adjusted to suit the experience you desire.

This freewill to make adjustments to our experience is what offers the varying shapes of the shadow. After creating us in His likeness, God gave us the freewill to make adjustments to our experience in limitless ways. In no way are any of us here on the Earth plane limited to making those adjustments, and in no way is any particular shape any one of us creates for ourselves right or wrong, either individually or as a whole. However, it is important to note that we are not limited to making those adjustments at any time in any moment.

Understanding this freewill to adjust is truly a secret to life. Like the analogy of the shower, we simply need to set the dial, or better stated "our intention," on the experience we so choose, and our shape, our experience, will adjust accordingly.

It is also as important to note that life takes place in the moment or "in the now." It is in these infinite moments of now that we have the freewill to make the adjustments to the temperature that suits our satisfaction. There is no need to wait, nor is there a need for haste. It can and will happen when we set our intention to our inner desire.

In this context, the term "desire" is used as a means for helping us understand our ability to make adjustments to get where we wish to be; the term is not being used here in the place of the term "want." However, we must understand that some may interpret the term "desire" as "to want," and to want is to assume we do not already have. To make this assumption, we inherently bring forth the opposite of what we want. Why? Because everything we could possibly want we already have. We just simply need to believe, and we shall achieve. If we are setting our intention on wanting something, wanting is what we shall get. Like a shower with a limitless flow of water and every possible temperature, we must come to realize that all we need to do is make adjustments and the limitless flow of water will adjust to the temperature that suits us appropriately. It is also important to realize that we may make adjustments at any given moment in time if what satisfies us "in the moment" suggests the change.

As I stood there, enjoying the temperature of the water that satisfied me in the moment, I began to ponder the thought that God and I are one. I am my own creator! When I wanted to make an adjustment to the temperature of the water, I simply needed to take action to make that adjustment. Knowing this helped me realize that I have this ability with every facet of my existence. And it isn't only an external force that I can adjust—an internal force could be just as easy. I have the freewill to think the way I choose to think, and feel the way I choose to feel. I can allow experiences to affect me in any way I wish.

I came to the understanding that I am the creator of my own experience. I can create whatever feels right for me. Granted, I might not necessarily be able to make myself taller or change the natural composition of my hair (yet), but I can certainly adjust the experience of each of those to a place where I can be satisfied with them. I can adjust the emotion associated with what I feel is dissatisfying about the experience. I can accept my outer Self the way it is and be satisfied and appreciative for simply being given the experience.

Having said that, I also realized there are things I can adjust if I prefer. I can modify my attitude. I can adjust my weight if it satisfies me in the moment. I simply need to set my intention on doing so—not wishing it to be or wanting it to be, but rather *intending* for it to happen, wholeheartedly and unconditionally. Only then will the adjustment be made. I cannot adjust the temperature of the shower if I don't intentionally reach my hand to the faucet and make the adjustment. Wishing or wanting the temperature to change would not change the temperature for me. The same can be said for any other adjustment we desire in life. We must take action!

A person with an ailment or a condition they are not satisfied with, such as a disease or dissatisfaction with weight, can and will only make the adjustment to their experience if they focus on it intentionally. As many may already know, intention is the key. We can set certain steps into motion to adjust to the experience that satisfies us, but if we set conditions to the experience we desire, we are not intending wholeheartedly. Therefore, the experience we desire may not be the result. I might not be able to adjust the temperature of the shower to the temperature that suits me if, before I reached up to the faucet, I set conditions to the process that is required to adjust the shower dial. For instance, I might not be able to move the dial to the desired temperature if I first set a condition in place where I can only move the dial in one direction. Therefore, it is Self who has the ability to make the adjustments without condition and is the creator of the experience of life.

Some beings may be more tapped into certain abilities than others, but that by no means suggests that each and every one of us cannot have exactly the same experience as another. For instance, I am a creative individual. I have tapped into my ability to create works of art and design. It is an ability I am very appreciative to have. I could also say that I do not posses the ability to remember things as well as others. However, recently I began to consider that quite possibly, I have set conditions to the process of my memory and have, therefore, not intentionally tried to remember all things. It is true that I can and do remember all things. I just have limited myself to only effectively recalling things I conveniently choose to recall.

Life is not always convenient. The changes we seek to our lives may very well require adjustments that are not satisfying in the interim. Imagine, if you will, the shower faucet offering the extremes of temperature—but not with the cold and hot extremes on each end. Consider what would happen if the temperature settings were hot and cold in varying points on the dial. In our adjustments, we may need to experience dissatisfying moments to achieve the results we desire. But, so long as our intention is true, we shall adjust to the experience that we find satisfying in the moment.

The result of my experience in the shower was the understanding that I can and must do what feels right for me in each moment of my life. Those around me for whom I may have concern will feel an effect from me making that adjustment, and will therefore make adjustments themselves for their own satisfying experience.

With freewill, we have the ability to do what feels right for each of us. We must consider that what we *think* would be satisfying in the end may not be the experience we expected. For instance, if we find that causing harm to another human being would be a satisfying experience, we could certainly make adjustments and set our intention on doing so. However, we also have the ability to have foresight, and having foresight, we can predict parts and pieces of the experience before we set our minds to doing so. In that prediction, we can play out possible outcomes and ongoing effects it may have on our and others' experience related to the intended experience we seek. We can continue to reconsider the outcome and make adjustments that finally give us satisfaction. In the end, the experience one may select may likely be to simply let go of the feelings they have toward the human being they wish to harm, because the resulting predicted possibilities for the experience may not be what would satisfy us. This is why truth in our intention plays such a key role in the adjustments of our experience. Without being true to ourselves, we cannot make the adjustments that will ultimately give us the satisfaction we seek.

Overcoming Limitations

As I have discussed previously in this book, much of our experience here is guided by limitations we set upon ourselves. These limitations are typically based on previous life experiences that shape our individual beliefs about what is achievable. It is funny, really: There are the laws of the universe, the laws of our governments, and the laws of our own beliefs. We understand many of the laws of these three systems, but there are others we do not understand. There are laws we practice daily, knowing full well what they are and why they may be necessary. Then there are the laws we practice without paying much attention or even realizing we practice them. But the reality is, the laws we set upon ourselves are there because we put them there. Governmental laws are created because we ask for them. Individual laws are created because we ask for them as well. It isn't until we start questioning our beliefs that we start to review the list of laws we have set for ourselves.

I had an experience back in 2007 that I wrote about in my journal, and like so many other journal entries, it made a great deal of sense to me. The entry was profound to me, and when I shared it with the public as an article, I received a great deal of feedback about its validity. It apparently made sense to quite a few individuals who read it, and because of this, I share it with you here.

Life Unlimited – Step Out of Life's Limitations

It was late. Having worked in the city for the afternoon and early evening, I found myself traveling home at dusk. The traffic had lightened, but the flashing taillights of a long line of commuters still resembled that of a Las Vegas video poker hall. I found my mind wandering in-and-out of a wide range of thoughts, ending in senseless oblivion: *When was that homeowner's association bill due?... When I refinanced that house, did I include the property tax in the payment, or is that a bill due next month?...I wonder what the guy in the car beside me is listening to. He seems to really like the tune...I wonder how they make reflectors work so well...Where are all these people going so late in the evening?...I wonder where we're going for my birthday. When was the last time the oil was changed?*

The top was down on the Jeep. The cool fall desert breeze trailed in and swirled around me with the occasional scent of catalytic converter emissions from vehicles before me. The bright city lights cast a pale glow overhead. Music pumped from the speakers of the Jeep, playing out a variety of tunes from the satellite radio stations as I searched for a song that would satisfy me in the moment. The car jerked about as the traffic sped up and then slowed abruptly off and on.

As I exited the freeway and began maneuvering my way out of the neighborhoods and toward my rural home, I found much of the day's stress begin to fade away, yet my thoughts still raced.

Passing through the last city stoplight on my journey and leaving behind the remaining string of city streetlights, I discovered the brilliance of the night sky. Brightly twinkling stars revealed themselves overhead. As the city glow faded, the stars shined brighter and brighter. With only a few miles remaining and travelers leaving me alone on the dark, winding road, I turned my head toward the sky. I was in awe.

As the Jeep tires hummed along against the pavement, I found the music that I had been listening to was now more of an irritation, so I turned it off. It was so peaceful that I found myself wanting to stare into the dark sky, exploring the millions of twinkling crystals. This, of course, was not an easy task while cruising along at fifty miles an hour. In this moment, my thoughts turned from the random nonsense we are all so familiar with in our day-to-day lives to something much more simple and appropriate. I set my mind free to enjoy the stars.

The experience of traveling along at fifty in a convertible while trying to remain focused on stars overhead can be a daunting task. Strangely, it revealed to me a very simple but often overlooked concept for living life.

Life, for most, is almost always lived like driving a car; focusing on the road, other drivers, animals, children playing ball, traffic signals, and so on. We spend so much time focusing on so many unnecessary elements of daily societal life that we often forget we are a tiny spec within such vast reality.

Like driving, life's experiences are often an unnecessary stress. Like driving, we find ourselves focused on hundreds of little components rather than enjoying the experience even for a moment. Like driving, the boredom and mundane routine often leads to the blurring together of the continuous experiences, to the point where we even fail to remember the overall experience we have been having. We have all done it before behind the wheel—driving along and then noticing that you don't even remember how you got to your destination. For many of us the experience of life passes us by in the same way.

As I looked to the sky, I found myself releasing all thoughts—releasing all the stresses of the day—yet I realized I could not simply look to the sky and drive at the same time. Therefore, I found myself needing to glance down at the road every few seconds. It was a very revealing experience. One moment I was at peace, and the next, I was back in the driving game—checking the speed, watching for wildlife, signs or for hidden police officers. It was unsettling.

I found myself wanting to spend more time looking up at the sky and less time on the road, but I knew that wasn't possible if I wanted to avoid veering off the road. I began to ponder the idea of fear. *Why am I so concerned about glancing down at the road? Why am I so concerned about the possibility of swerving off the road to my sudden death? And yet a better question, if I really want to gaze at the stars, why don't I just pull over? It isn't like I am pressed for time to get somewhere.*

At a time in one's life when the process of connecting to inner Self, your spiritual Self, begins to occur, the experience is much like the analogy of driving the car. We find ourselves spending more time in that realm of thought, and it begins to "interfere" with the daily life we have surrounded ourselves with until we experience a shift. Rather, our daily life begins to interfere with this new thought process of "really living." Once this shift takes place, we begin to see that we can no longer accept many of the components of the reality in which we have submersed ourselves. We begin to see that the structure of society we have selected to live within is no longer valid for us. Elements of control, judgment of Self and others, being taught to cope with rather than release pains of the past, actually creating the reality we want rather than simply accepting the one we have, releasing fear and living free from it rather than living under its thumb—these and so many other aspects of society begin to create so many questions in our minds.

As time goes on and we begin to grow, it becomes more and more important to find answers to these questions. Why? Because they do not mesh with the true reality of why we are here. Yes, we are here to learn, and we do so through experiences —experiences we may categorize in our societal lives as "good" or "bad." But the reality is that the experience is neither good nor bad. It is just that, an experience. Once we have learned what we feel we must from such an experience, we learn we may simply choose to move on from it and are then able to release it. As we grow, many of the elements of societal life tend to no longer jive with who we are in the moment. This, to me, is a sure sign of spiritual growth.

But this growth is not always easy. In fact, others around you may not understand why you are no longer willing to accept their control, their judgment, their fear, their constant ramblings of past pain, their egocentric ways, their constant need for pity, co-dependency, lack of self-discipline (or more appropriately, lack of love for the Self enough not to abuse it), their need to pass off responsibility for their own actions to another (taking them out of the driver's seat of their own life), and so many other tendencies of our society.

Once you begin to experience this, you know you are on your way to really living life. To really live life, you must focus on Self. Society sees this as selfishness, but I see it like so many of our respected pioneers of this way of life do—as "self-ishness," centered on Self and not self-centeredness. Only when we see life in this way can we really make strides with our growth. Only when we experience life in this way are we self-empowered. Only when we are self-empowered will we begin to create our lives rather than our lives being created for us. Many authors refer to this as "consciously creating." Only when you are completely aware that you have the ability to create will your life begin to adjust to what you desire. Don't fear self-ishness! Know that one who is centered on Self realizes that to love others, one must first love thyself. A master of the art of Self understands that adverse actions toward another is really an adverse act toward Self, because all is one.

When we do this without fear, we will realize that all things and everyone around us will adjust to the new version of ourselves, and as a result, we and everyone around us benefits. They may not see it this way to begin with, but eventually they will get it. Eventually they will see that we made these adjustments as improvements and expansions of ourselves.

So, the next time you are driving along in stressful traffic or find yourself submersed in the intricacies of daily societal life and its routines, stop and become aware of the matter. Assess the importance of the tasks at hand. Compare that to the real tasks you have put yourself in this experience for. Seize the moment and allow the profoundness of thought to shape the experience and help provide you focus on what is really important. For me, living life in this way is to live life "unlimited."

Expressing Ourselves Openly

I am a supporter of equality. I believe we each have our own paths to follow, and along those various winding paths are great learning experience for each of us. Conscious creation is based on utilizing creativity purposefully. To create, we must be expressive. When I was in high school, I found myself wanting to express myself creatively, and in doing so, I stood out from time to time with the way I dressed, the way I cut and styled my hair, and the music I listened to. What I experienced then, in the microcosm of the high school peer society, helped me to understand the limitations we put on ourselves out of fear of being accepted by others.

The reality is, though, if it weren't for great visionaries who step outside common belief, our society would simply not be experiencing the exponential growth we encounter today. As I faced this whole concept of awakening, I discovered that, though I was by far not alone, there is a large majority that still considers this process to be "not of the norm." However, by observing this, I also realized I was beginning to unplug from the artificial system that commercialism has instilled in us all from our birth. Yes, the visionaries have created seemingly great improvements in our societal lives, but the entrepreneurs have also capitalized on our limited knowledge at the same time, and this has led to a belief system of artificial expression.

Case in point is a journal entry I wrote in 2007, which I titled "To Really Express." I felt compelled to express my thoughts about how we relate to expression, and what it really means to openly express ourselves. Expression starts from within, and the resulting experience—all that matters—is simply love.

To Really Express

I find it such a turn-off to step into the grocery store at the end of December and see displays of Valentine's candy, gifts, and cards. It seems the only tradition left in

America is the push for Americans to spend money at every turn in order to show outward expression of love or appreciation for another.

They say that Valentine's Day is a special day set aside to show your dearest love how much you care for them, and that you appreciate the love they have for you.

Let us consider for a moment that in order to love another human being, you must first love yourself. In order to love the reality in which we currently reside, you must first love yourself as an experience within that reality. Outward expression starts from the inside, and appreciation for others starts with appreciation for Self.

When considering how the law of attraction relates to relationships, we must first consider that we attract experiences based on the expressions (the vibrations) that radiate from our core being.

I have a friend who is currently quite frustrated with his love life. In his early forties, he is tired of being alone and longs for a deeply loving relationship. From my perspective, he is a great guy who would give anyone the shirt off his back. He has a great sense of humor, is quite adventurous, and is in a place in his life where he desires real heartfelt experiences. I hear from him now and then, and it seems his typical experience when meeting girls is to get serious very quickly, even on the first date. Even before the first date, he sets himself up for loss, stating, "If this one doesn't work out it is going to be a long time before I recover." He puts off a very particular vibration from his core being that seems to repel the potential relationship time and time again. Quite possibly, he attracts that experience to begin with!

Before my friend can find that love in someone else, he must first turn inward. He must realize that to find someone that satisfies him or is satisfied with him, he must first be satisfied with himself. Only then will he put off the energy in his life to attract what he is looking for.

Some say the only way we know we exist is by the reflection of Self that we see in those around us. For instance, without language, we could not communicate. Without communication, we could not generate dialog that we can use to evaluate and eventually sculpt our existence. This seems like a very outward way of looking at life, and I for one am not so convinced this is the case. However, if all things are one, then this concept does make some sense.

I'm not so sure this concept is my reality, but I do feel what relationships bring to our existence seems more appealing than being here without another to experience it with.

So, what is it to really express love? I believe the greatness of love lies within the notion that we are all things, and to love Self is to love all things... but also, to love all things is to love Self. Remember... you ARE all things.

This Valentine's Day, consider expressing your love for yourself. Then, once you feel content with doing so, express love for all things that exist in your reality. Finally, express appreciation for being given an opportunity to experience this reality to begin with. Whether you are happy in your experience within this reality or not, you are here. That, in itself, is an amazing thing to consider.

Regardless of what is going on in your life, appreciate it for what it is—an experience. Rest assured that if you have someone in your life that you consider to be extra special, they are there because you feel that way about yourself. That person sees in you what you see in you.

If you have someone in your life you consider to be your partner and that person is not satisfactory to you, consider that person a reflection of you. It is you that is in need of your attention before you can correct your outward relationship woes.

So, to truly express to your dearest (outward) love, give them a big hug. And, when doing so, believe from your deepest knowing that you are expressing love for yourself.

If you do not have a special someone in your life, consider making that special someone YOU! While I'm not positive of it, I am pretty sure that when you truly do this, a reflection of Self will appear before your outward-looking eyes.

Toning and Tuning

Once I learned a greater understanding of how we seemingly form into our physical selves through vibrational frequencies—which are really just sounds—it clicked for me how sound could be used to manipulate our physical existence. I was then introduced to toning and tuning as a means for resonating harmoniously with Nature. With this understanding, it became very clear to me that we should also be able to create that harmony within our bodies. After all, disease is dis-harmony. What if we could project our voices in a particular tone with the intention of healing ourselves? And, assuming all is one, what would stop us from being able to create harmony within the seemingly physical body of another? This is something I firmly believe. We can heal ourselves. Through conscious thought, positive focus, and using our intuition to uncover the dis-harmony, we can utilize vibration to restore harmony where harmony was once lost.

What better tool do we have than our own voices for creating healing tones and tunes? Utilizing good, healing intent, a heart filled with love, and a consistent tone, our own vocal cords can be the most powerful instrument ever projected into this reality.

Toning is actually quite easy, and I must say it can generate a number of very interesting results. I have participated in one-on-one toning, as well as group toning sessions. There is NOTHING quite like lying on a table and having fifteen people toning over you, all with the intent of healing you with their hearts filled with love. In my one-on-one experience, I felt a deep, caring connection with the person I was working on.

In fact, I recall on one occasion, I had been conducting a toning session on a fellow classmate. My intuition told me she held a great deal of angst in her feet. She was lying on a massage table before me. I proceeded to tone near her feet and projected my voice in a consistent tune. My intention was to help her release the emotional trauma she might be holding on to. After I toned for about five minutes, she began to cry. After working with her to release an experience from her past, we discussed what she had felt during the toning process. She shared that she became consumed with a level of harmony, love, and peace that she had not felt in a long time. She realized just how much power her haunting past had over her—all of which she apparently held in her feet. Interestingly, both of her feet were fairly deformed, and only three weeks earlier, she had recovered from two—yes, two!—accidents involving her feet.

Belief

There are few things in this reality more powerful than belief. On more than one occasion, I have witnessed examples in which individuals who were diagnosed with some sort of disease (some life threatening and others just annoyances) were able to heal themselves. How? Through ongoing self-healing efforts and a solid core belief that they *could* heal themselves. In both cases, doctors had told the individuals that they would suffer for the rest of their lives, but through determination and commitment to the goal, they overcame and left doctors questioning how.

I believe in this power. There is nothing quite like having a fundamental belief in something. It is a seed that plants real strength, perseverance, and the will to beat the odds. We could all use a little more core belief in something. The adage, "Believe and you can achieve" holds true. There isn't a life coach I know who doesn't teach this in their practice. It is often the foundation for which all success is reached in whatever endeavor one pursues.

Intuition

Understanding my own intuitive cues changed a

lot of my life perspectives. We all have the ability to *feel* a sense about things. Knowing how to evaluate that intuitive feeling is the difference between acknowledging that feeling and understanding it. Many of us make decisions about things without proper due diligence. However, a better understanding of what gut feelings really mean can make all the difference in a decision that serves you and one that doesn't. Though my intuitive understanding is, at this point, underdeveloped, I will certainly acknowledge that it has evolved significantly. In particular, the Intuitive Powers Practical Applications courses I mentioned earlier gave me the opportunity to learn how to utilize my intuition not only for my own benefit, but also for the benefit of others. I was able to learn how to read other peoples' bodies, find where they are experiencing pain, and help them release whatever it is that they are holding onto that is causing the ailment. Some of us are born with a natural ability to be intuitive. Others are not even aware we have such tools available to us. It is up to you to nurture this ability.

Meditation

As I have discussed in other parts of *Rediscovering Your Divine Music*, meditation has offered me countless amazing experiences. Stripping away everything but slow, deep breaths can find us with an opportunity to finally, truly know our higher Self.

If you have yet to try meditation, I highly recommend it as the primary tool for reconnecting to your divine music. Meditation can take place just about anywhere. It doesn't have to take much time. I have meditated for five minutes at times and have still received the peace that was needed at the moment. On other occasions, my meditations have lasted up to an hour, or even more. It all depends on you. In any case, you may meditate with your eyes closed or open. You can focus on a candle flame, on darkness, or deep into the landscape horizon. I have even meditated facing another individual, and in doing so, I have seen their face shift right before my eyes. I couldn't believe it! The face shifted from the person I recognized into an old woman with a hooded veil over her head. She was in such sorrow that it brought tears to my eyes.

Take time for yourself to meditate alone, or ask your partner to spend time each evening, or at least a few times per week, to really experience the peace that meditation can bring to your life. It can also be an opportunity to meet people. We have held group meditations before, hosting as many as thirty people for one-hour meditation classes. Afterwards, we have always had a discussion to share what we had experienced as a group. Group meditation can be a great way to meet like-minded individuals, and having scheduled meetings will keep meditation a part of your busy schedule.

Don't underestimate the power of meditation.

This book, the company Token Rock, my relationships, and the happy, fulfilled life path I now walk are all a direct result of the meditation I gave to myself atop that mountain years ago following my father's transition. Having given myself that moment of peace, I was able to find what really mattered in my life.

Fresh Air

Nothing on Earth is more effective than finding yourself in the clean air and peace of Nature. Giving yourself that experience—along with some of these other very effective tools such as meditation, toning, intentions, positive thinking and manifestation in Nature – can be incredibly powerful.

After a rainstorm, I can't help but want to go outside and take a deep breath. I love the feel of the bright sun after a deluge and the smell of the rain on the plants, trees, and soil. There is something very refreshing and harmonious about breathing a deep breath of fresh air. Our indoor air quality is poor at best, unless you have a costly air purification system in your home or office—and even then, it is not the same as Nature. Ever notice how plants react better to rain than to sprinkler heads? At least they do in my yard. I find that my plants sprout new shoots and the grass grows faster with rainfall, while they respond much less effectively with the treated water from the city water system. Your own body is no different. You are the plants and trees! Treat yourself to the same reward. Energize yourself with a day in Nature. Get out of the city if at all possible and sit among the tall grasses on a rolling hillside. Take a quiet walk on a vacant beach. Sit on a boulder along a running stream. Hear the breeze blowing and the leaves quaking. Get out and treat yourself!

Opening the Door to Your Creativity

Earlier in my life, there were people close to me who would tell me that, creative individuals are hard to live with. Maybe they were right, though I'm not exactly sure why this is. Possibly it's because my mind is constantly processing, conjuring up new ideas and concepts. I'm not one to embrace limitations. I prefer to grow and expand whenever possible.

As a result, often, if one notices me gazing off into the distance and asks what I am thinking about, I return with about a half hour of random scenarios and scenes. "Well, I was thinking about this, and this led me to think about that..." and so on. It is just a part of me, who I am.

Years have gone by now, and my home scenery has changed. I have found myself living in a household of creative individuals. My wife, all of my children, and I are all highly creative.

Recently, I found myself pondering a host of

random thoughts. This time, though, I was admiring the level of creativity that illuminates our home on a daily basis. It was the weekend and I had just completed a new design before deciding to take a break. As I wandered around the house, I discovered Carrie-Anne working on her CD recording in our oldest son's room, since he is a musician and has a recording studio set up in there. I found my oldest writing a new song and playing it on his guitar in the courtyard, and I later happened upon one of my other sons sitting at the kitchen table, drawing pictures. I take a great deal of satisfaction and appreciation that my home is filled with such creative people—and I most certainly don't think they are hard to live with. In fact, it's quite the contrary!

What does it mean to be creative? Why do some find themselves naturally creative and others do not? What can you do to open the door to your creativity? These are questions I feel that are begging to be answered.

What Does It Mean to Be Creative?

First of all, we must realize that in one way or another, every one of us is creative. There is not a soul here in this reality today that isn't. We all create each and every day. In fact, we cannot awaken each morning without being creative. Every moment and every step forward requires creativity. But, what does this mean?

What it comes down to is focus. If, in each and

every single moment of our existence here we are all constantly creating, it becomes a matter of what we create in the moment. We are ALL artists and designers of our own lives.

I fully understand the possible fear some may experience when putting a paintbrush or pencil to a blank canvas. Many are afraid they will fail—that their work of art will be a train wreck. The reality is that a train wreck *is* only just that when the creator believes it to be. Remember, many artists become famous only after they have been put six feet under. Take Picasso or Andy Warhol, for instance. In my personal opinion, neither of these artists produced work that was groundbreaking or masterful, but that is simply my own opinion. Look how their work shaped many individuals' perspectives and inspired others to create.

I can't confirm it, but I would gather that it wasn't about popularity for Picasso when he created his first works. I'm guessing he simply put paintbrush to paper and called it art in his own mind. The funny thing about Warhol is that he probably could have literally painted a train wreck and sold it. In his mind, maybe what he felt he was creating was a work of art. So, what it boils down to is that it is about your own personal beliefs. Do you fear a blank canvas? Do you believe wholeheartedly that you lack a single creative bone in your body? I am sorry to have to tell you this, but it just isn't true. Whether you know it or not, you are just as masterful at this creativity thing as Michelangelo. If you're thinking, *The creatives are over there, and I am over here,* it's all in your head, my friend! You and "the creatives" are one in the same!

Being creative is simply a thought process that puts you at the turning wheel. It is a conscious decision to care not what others may think of the clay pot you shape with your bare hands. Society needs not be your limitation when creating a work of art. You ARE society, and I assure you, *being* society, the only limitation is you.

Why Do Some Find Themselves Naturally Creative While Others Do Not?

Regardless of the various excuses or confirmations each of us conjure up (*"Oh, he's a Libra... it says here he is creative!"*), one is no more creative than the next. This may help ease the thought process, but as I mentioned, we are ALL creative. The only difference is that some may have an easier time translating a thought about an image into brain commands, thus instructing our hand to put it on paper. Coordination between the brain and the hand may be the only hurdle, but it certainly doesn't mean ART wasn't created.

But art isn't all about painting and drawing. It is music, sculpture, culinary, dance, writing, gardening, hedge trimming, poetry, public speaking, whispering in your partner's ear, dog grooming, making Mickey Mouse pancakes in the frying pan, how you put your catsup and mustard on your hot dog, the order in which you keep your desk, smiling for photographs, how you write, the experiences you create in your day-to-day life... and the list goes on into infinity. We are all creative in our own way. In fact, *diversity is creativity*. Again, though, it all comes down to one's frame of mind. Don't cast away creatives. Don't classify creative individuals apart from any other so-called group. No matter how analytical you may consider your thinking and brain to be, you are just as creative as anyone else. Embrace it! If you feel you have creative block, find a way to overcome it. Focus on it... just start doing it NOW!

What Can You Do to Open the Door to Your Creativity?

Try this. Put your brain on autopilot. Close your eyes. Allow your mind to wander. Put an idea in your head and follow it around a bit. See where it goes. Venture down any path your wandering mind may want to explore. Give it about ten minutes. Then open your eyes and write down everything you can recall from the experience. Don't be concerned about what it was you thought about. The random concepts, translated into words on paper, are your first example of how your own creative process works. It's that simple.

As I mentioned earlier, my son is a musician, and he plays instruments very well. He has no formal training. He writes music and lyrics and then records his work. People say he is gifted, but what I see is focus. He is a young man who has made it a priority to play music well. He practices every day, and no one has to tell him to do it. It is automatic for him because he loves it. He loves creating something new. Creativity is addicting. The more you believe in your ability to create, the more you make a conscious choice to do it.

I love my creative family. It inspires me to walk around my home and see people creating. I think it brings me back to my college days. I remember walking the campus at school and feeling the energy. People were there to learn... on purpose! Inquiring minds wanted to know, and we were all there for the same reason. It didn't matter the subjects or the departments. It was a place of new ideas where people were on an upward path to wherever they wanted to head in life. That is how I feel in my home when I walk around and see these individuals practicing their music, recording a CD, drawing the next creative scene, or listening to them try to make even the faintest squeak from a school band clarinet like my nine-year old has been making attempts to do. It is ALL music to me.

Every aspect of Nature and the natural process of life is creativity in the making. It is all a harmony of music, and in my home, the music plays loud and clear. The melody plays out in the smell of homemade bread that my boys spend time making... even when the kitchen is a disaster afterward. Harmony plays out in the beautiful water feature my wife built for the wildlife to drink from this past weekend... even when I had to get out there and help her in 112-degree heat. It is now something to marvel at and enjoy, especially when quail congregate around it gratefully.

It was her willingness to set aside the limitations and get out there and do it. It was her desire to translate the thought in her mind into the commands to the hands to carry out the task to create—to express herself through her creative work. Now, because of her efforts, this new instrument is added to the harmonious music. The animals will enjoy the water resource, we will enjoy the animals, and in the end, that enjoyment will spark new ideas... and the creativity, the harmonious symphony of melodies, will continue to flow.

Though we fail to realize it, this is a process we are all masters of. We are instruments of creativity. Creation is an ongoing process in which we each play an integral part. We can choose what we create. What will you create to add to the divine music that plays in each and every moment? What will you shape and mold with the energy of this world? It is there, waiting to be shaped. The possibilities are limitless. You just need to walk over and sit down at the turning wheel and put your hands on that lump of clay. Feel its smooth texture.

Sink your hands into its cool depths... or walk up to the microphone, type to your heart's content, or express in some way that only you know will satisfy your creativity. *Be who you were put here to be… a creator indeed!*

Sonoran Symphony

The sun pokes through the morning haze
Upon the desert I gently gaze

Atop this cliff I find my place
Upon Mother Earth in all her grace

The astounding beauty of this new day
Lets Nature's music softly play

The desert slope on mountains high
Reaches beyond the clear blue sky

Here I sit on a massive bould'
Pondering many myths that I've been told

Green desert giants surround my perch
Reasons for their being I shall always search

A gentle breeze blows across my ear
The silence knows no sound to hear

The abounding Nature so alive and free
Fills the heart inside of me

~ SC Leuthold

Chapter 7

TAKING OFF THE TRAINING WHEELS

Giving Myself the Gift of Love

A Self-Help Story with a Twist

I've read a number of self-help books in my day and have yet to find one with a story that ends with a twist. This one does. It took me almost two-and-a-half years to write the content of this book, and in the process, the life lessons gave me the stories I wished to share. I had put the book away for almost eight months with the belief that it was incomplete, that I had more lessons to learn before it could be finished. There was a chapter missing—and that chapter was this one.

It wasn't until I started writing this chapter that it hit me why I had to wait for it to be experienced. My life had come full circle. One afternoon in the midst of the experience this chapter is about, I began to feel the desire to write. As I opened the book file and started writing, I felt compelled to pause and return to the beginning of the book and read it through. I wanted to fully submerse myself in the story so I could feel that I really had my head around the magnitude of the message.

As I read the pages one by one, the feelings of fear and doubt began to surface. These uneasy feelings were far too familiar, particularly in recent months, and now I completely understood why. The stories of my own life, moving on from one relationship to another to find that "true love" or just simply for change, were surfacing once again, but this time I wasn't the one searching. This time, I was on the receiving end. I soon realized that what I feared most was having my love partner read this book. Not that she isn't already aware of what is talked about on these pages; she has plenty of knowledge herself about the concepts I've written, and she certainly knows the stories of my life. This was about confirmation. There was no way I could deny her everything she had been seeking. Even if she hadn't ever read the book, I could no longer deny in my own mind what it was she was experiencing. I had been there before, so I knew I was in for major growth within myself. A realization surfaced that a balance between outward and inward love is my lesson in life, and that giving of myself needs to be universal.

Loving Me

The power of change will always find its way into our minds, even when we think we have reached our goals. Even when we feel we have achieved all that we set out to achieve, we are provided yet another angle from which to view our experience.

My pursuit to find true happiness from within led me down such an amazing path of self-discovery, but during the process, I focused so heavily on finding true outward love. Doing so proved to be yet another life lesson—one I would soon have the opportunity to learn a great deal from.

This phase of my experience came as an enormous shock to my thought process. I was deeply in love. I had reached what I thought to be the peak of a mountain that I had spent nearly 20 years of my life trying to ascend. I had planted the flag at the top and was happy with my love relationship. Yes, I felt I had made a number of sacrifices in an effort to have the experience, but my belief at the time was that it was well worth it. In spite of my contentment, as the summertime monsoon arrived in the southwest desert, so, too, came a perfect storm in my life.

Though I was apparently suppressing discontentment in some aspects and had fear in others, it was surely overshadowed by my deep love for my partner. Then reality struck, and life threw me a major curve ball.

I discovered that no matter how deeply I was in love with my partner, I couldn't control my partner's reciprocal feelings. It became clear to me, though at the time I was in denial, that my love for Carrie-Anne was largely given conditionally. I had entered and conducted myself in our relationship with expectations and assumptions that she would return the favor by validating me, showing me the same actions in return. As midsummer passed, it became clear that we were set adrift on a new path. The only question was: would that path be traveled together or apart?

It wasn't that we didn't love one another. Each of us had grown more while being together than we had in all the years of our lives prior. It wasn't that we wanted to go our separate ways, either. The elephant in the room was the desire for personal growth—independently. That wasn't what I thought I wanted, so I immediately resisted. In fact, I headed down this path kicking and screaming. I had allowed myself to become consumed by the relationship. It became a bit of a rollercoaster ride, but amidst the ups and downs, loops and curves, we also found peace and solace in being together at times. Though there was a significant amount of tension, we also found a great deal of time to share our real thoughts, feelings, and emotions. There were times we simply didn't talk and other times when we allowed the door to swing wide open to have the deepest of conversations.

Then, during an evening out with a few friends, I came to realize that maybe I had created this entire experience. Maybe my subconscious was reminding me of my initial intent, of finding true happiness from within. My partner was clearly a reflection of me and was quite possibly expressing herself as a reflection of what I wasn't willing to admit. My love was so powerful for this individual that I had shut my eyes to the fact that, I, too, had forgone my independent nature in exchange for the beautiful love relationship we had created. I soon discovered that I had a lot of fear about "losing" the one I had so desperately sought in my life. But why?

Still being dragged kicking and screaming toward reality, the revelation slowly began to change my perspective. *What about loving me? As the Libra I truly am, have I neglected loving myself for complete outward love?* Not entirely, but certainly quite significantly. Then I began to let go of the fear. I began to embrace me. I began to take a few moments here and there to contemplate my true happiness. It was true. I wasn't taking care of me, nor was I being honest about my conditions of the relationship. I wondered how I could free myself from the fear-based emotions associated with my connection with my partner, still love her, and allow her to love me in her own way, all while simultaneously making room to love myself.

In our conversations, I began to question why I had such profound love for her and not the same love for myself. I contemplated what it would be like if everyone on Earth could love themselves and others around them with the deepest of compassion and without expectations. This is where my entire journey began to come full circle.

I discovered that in my relentless charge forward to find true love, I had forgotten where true love begins and ends. It was me who was seeking love, but it was also me who was poised to accept *my* love. I was waiting patiently, knowing that one day I would come to realize whom I truly needed to love. I began to establish a knowing that I had found the true love I had always been looking for, and it was right inside of me all along. I had found compassion and respect for myself, and with this newfound partnership, I was able to release Carrie-Anne from my gripping hold. I thought that through the experience, our relationship might grow to a profoundly deeper level—that freeing ourselves might actually instill the desire to continue walking parallel paths more profoundly than ever.

My life had changed forever. I arrived at a realization that though I had always talked about balance, I had rarely (at least in this love relationship) included a vital part of the equation: loving me. It had been an addiction to outward love, and as such, I had neglected myself. In my own life, I hadn't really wholeheartedly embraced or applied everything I had learned; the things I have shared with you in previous chapters.

Reading page after page, I came to realize that what I had written was written for *me* to read. I had scribed my very own self-help book. The words spoke to me unlike anything I had read before and gave me perspectives I could certainly relate to and comprehend. *Rediscovering Your Divine Music* was my very own lighthouse for which I could use to navigate home.

The Words of a Master

One evening I found myself home, lying in bed alone, reflecting on the current state of things and asking aloud for clarity and a release. As I lay in the darkness in contemplation, I began to think about a new book I wanted to write. Wondering how I could approach the concept for the book, I got out of bed and walked in the darkness into my living room. Asking again for clarity, I walked toward my library and turned on the chandelier. I walked straight over to my bookshelf and focused my attention on the first book I saw there, *The Prophet* by Kahlil Gibran. When I pulled the book from the shelf and flipped through the pages, a greeting card fell out —one Carrie-Anne had given to me years ago. I opened the card and read the message: "One person can make all the difference – and that person is YOU." She shared with me her love and her appreciation for the journey we'd shared and for allowing us to both grow in our own way. I read the pages of the book where the card had been placed, and in doing so, I received the message I had been seeking:

> *"Your soul is oftentimes a battlefield, upon which your reason and your judgment wage war against your passion*

and your appetite.

Would that I could be the peacemaker in your soul, that I might turn the discord and the rivalry of your elements into oneness and melody.

But, how shall I, unless you yourself be also the peacemakers, nay, the lovers of all your elements..."

I must love myself! Then, as I flipped the pages further, my eye caught a segment that was a clear reminder. The message had been read aloud at our wedding. I had forgotten how profound the words were when we had selected them together as a representation of our vows:

Love gives naught but itself and takes naught but from itself.

Love possesses not nor would it be possessed;

For love is sufficient unto itself.

When you love you should not say, 'God is in my heart,' but rather, 'I am in the heart of God.'

And think not you can direct the course of love, for love, if it finds you worthy, directs your course.

Love has no other desire but to fulfill itself.

But if you love and must needs have desires, let these be your desires:

To melt and be like a running brook that sings its melody to the night;

To know the pain of too much tenderness;

To be wounded by your own understanding of love;

And to bleed willingly and joyfully;

To wake at dawn with a winged heart and give thanks for another day of loving;

To rest at the noon hour and meditate love's ecstasy;

To return home at eventide with gratitude;

And then to sleep with a prayer for the beloved in your heart and a song of praise upon your lips.

Then Almitra spoke again and said, 'And what of marriage, Master?'

And he answered, saying:

'You were born together, and together you shall be forevermore.

You shall be together when the white wings of death scatter your days.

Ay, you shall be together in the silent memory of God.

But let there be spaces in your togetherness,

And let the winds of the heavens dance between you.

Love one another, but make not a bond of love:

Let it rather be a moving sea between the shores of your souls.

Fill each other's cup, but drink not from one cup.

Give one another of your bread, but eat not from the same loaf.

Sing and dance together and be joyous, but let each one of you be alone,

Even as the strings of a lute are alone though they quiver with the same music.

Give your hearts, but not into each other's keeping.

For only the hand of Life can contain your hearts.

And stand together, yet not too near together:

For the pillars of the temple stand apart,

And the oak tree and the cypress grow not in each other's shadow."

~ Kahlil Gibran, *The Prophet*

Understanding Love, Life's Ultimate Purpose

So, what is love? To be frank, this entire book comes down to this question's answer. My journey, as it turns out, has been, and continues to be, to discover just how deep love goes. To me, understanding what love is answers everything. Now, clearly any psychologist would suggest that love is an emotion and not just any emotion, but arguably life's most intense emotion that can be literally expressed in infinite ways. I couldn't agree more. But, fundamentally, love to me far surpasses the classification of a human emotion. From my perspective, emotion is a term that describes an energetic vibration. In its most profound state, I view love as the supporting pillar of our existence. At the center of everything I believe we find pure light. So, this being the case, I believe love isn't simply an experience in our lives, it ***is*** our lives. Love is what describes that which all life was miraculously created from. Embracing this realization and opening our hearts to sharing in such an experience offers us a glimpse into who we truly are. A life committed to mastering love is a life lived with clear purpose.

Science has largely avoided the research of love. Our emotions of fear and anger can be more easily tracked and measured, yet, love is something much less measurable. Science is founded on research that can be quantified and proven, whereas love can often only be justly described with creative expression. That is if we view love as the comforting, joyful, tender emotion that it certainly is.

I find that searching for life's unanswered questions takes me swirling into endless spirals. The answer to one question creates a thousand more questions. Yet, those spirals send me whirling around a nucleus of truth. At the center of the energetic atom that is our existence we find the wholeness that is pure, unwavering love. It is our destiny to return here, to where we originated. It is our destiny to return to love.

Here in reality, we struggle to find our truth. We battle our relentless egos. We ask for life challenges to conquer in order to learn and grow, but for what if not to chart a course back to the pure innocence of love that we truly are?

Young Love

As we enter this reality, many of us first experience love as newborn infants from hopeful, protective parents who care for our every need. This often is a very unconditional love experience. As we grow and mature, these love relationships shape the person we are to become. The experiences in this phase of our lives imprint upon our subconscious and, as we mature, reflect how we've perceived these moments as we advance forward. The perspectives we shape about this powerful emotion at this impressionable age span our lifetimes, creating both doorways and barriers to our understanding of love.

At some point in our youth, many of us are exposed to our first *special love* experience. This wildy passionate fixation on our first love is often considered an infatuation, yet, this relationship introduces us to so many emotions and valuable life lessons. These relationships open the door to a taste for love, although we have yet to really understand what it is that we crave. The gamut of feelings are expressed and reciprocated and these feelings set the stage for how we perceive love and our quest to experience more of it.

Relationship and Special Love

Entering adulthood, many of us move along our journey toward special relationships and discover a serious and profound level of love that far surpasses any love experience we've felt prior. Thus, we merge lives into one intertwined experience and establish a union of our hearts, minds, and souls with another human being. However, we often have much to learn about ourselves still, let alone about the emotional bond of love. Some of these relationships succeed, others, as so often is experienced here in the west, fail. We do learn from our experiences but patterns that have been established from young love and on through our adulthood plague our lives, leading to repeat failures. But why? Why does this happen so often and why has it become so prevalent in our society? There are many reasons, of course, why the divorce rate has skyrocketed. One might say that divorce was just not an acceptable method of resolution in our historical past like it has become today. We might also consider that, as generations mature, they also evolve and with this evolution, commitment just isn't taught as it once was. It could be that with the advancement of technology and a society where everything is at our fingertips immediately we just have lost patience for the union of love. We want change and we want it regularly to keep life new and exciting. Because our brains are used to constant stimulation it could be that we just simply get bored.

I can't deny that humanity is always evolving. Both men and women just aren't limiting themselves to the domestic roles they once were. Life for so many just seems to have lost deep meaning and connection in exchange for superficial, artificial and materialistic (SAM) experiences. But, with evolution, not all is lost. Much is often gained. At some point in our quest for the SAM experience we begin to realize that our lives are incomplete—that we long for something much more meaningful. And, thus, we begin to search for something—anything—that will fill the void that the SAM experience often leaves us with.

Sex, Intimacy, and Love

Oh, the joys of sex. The confusion of love in our youth relationships is that we associate sex with love. There is a big difference to me between sex and intimacy and typically, it seems, our young relationships are more about physical attraction than they are about love. Passion is first sparked in these early days of our lives through these relationships and, because we lack the experience to see things any differently, physical attraction becomes deeply tied to our vision of love. This vision often establishes the patterns that create the relationship failures.

So is sex a part of love? Of course it is. If it weren't it wouldn't be an option in our experience. Intercourse is the source of creating life on Earth. However, in my opinion there are very different levels to love as an emotion and two partners can experience a deeply profound connection made through intimate sexuality. I do separate sex from intimacy. I believe that the carnal passion of sexual seduction is a valuable experience for two individuals to share. There is nothing wrong with it in my mind. However, the emotional experience of it does not necessarily bring us any closer to our understanding of what love really is. Sex on its own is a physical stimuli not always associated with a heart and mind connection. Is it fulfilling? In some ways, yes, however, not always do we find what we are really looking for once the passion passes.

Monogamy in the New Paradygm

So, what do we tend to do in order to achieve the fulfillment that sex alone has not provided? We strive to find love and when we think we have found it, we explore its depths. But, rather than remaining individually whole and complete, we create a bond of love. I am no stranger to doing just this in relationships. I have learned through trial and error that a bond of love is not the true nature of emotional love. This has been a deeply challenging realization to accept. How do we remain ourselves and allow our partner to remain themselves while building a powerful special love relationship when we are engulfed in the ego's fear and jealousy, causing us to set conditions on love? This stems from deeply rooted experiences that have imprinted their pain and suffering on our lives. It is here that we can make the greatest advancements in our quest to truly understand love. Working to face and release these traumatic experiences paves the way to unshackling ourselves from the repeating patterns that hinder our true understanding of love. We begin to see how the bond of love has established an unhealthy attachment and addiction to the experience of special relationship love.

Self Love

As we begin to see the patterns and make the connection between them and the past that guides our present, we unlock the door to a deep love connection with the special love in our life. It is here that we finally begin to understand the meaningful experience that special love offers. However, if we have not truly come to love ourselves, we will tend to have a difficult time fully sharing ourselves with another. We find that to truly share ourselves with another we must first know who we are, accept who we are, and embrace all that makes us unique. This is often what continues to challenge the success of our special love relationships. We try time and time again to get it right, but until we take a good hard look in the mirror evaluating what makes one's Self tick, giving wholeheartedly to another is simply impossible.

This is where I feel humanity is beginning to spiritually awaken. In our rapid evolution, we are starting to take pause before jumping into special love relationships with another in exchange for beginning to truly fall in love with ourselves. Or, if we are in relationships, many are beginning to come to the realization that we must take a step backward to take two steps forward. It is often difficult to see that our partner is doing us a favor by taking pause and reflecting on the feelings they have. After all, how can they truly love you when they may not fully understand or love themselves? I see humanity's spiritual evolution moving toward Self love. I believe we will see a continued escalation of divorce and fewer and fewer couples marrying in exchange for holding on to personal power. I believe couples will share in special love but from the vantage point of first fulfilling Self love, and then sharing in a relationship. However, I do not see it ending here. I do believe that over time, humanity will find a place for deeply loving special relationships, but I do question if there is a place for special love in a paradigm of global oneness. It is difficult to see where special love may fit into a world where we strive to love each other deeply and profoundly without condition, without the bond of love. If we can truly begin to let go of the ego's control over our emotions and, in exchange, share in love without conditions, could we possibly no longer need special relationships? Could monogamy become a worn out practice that simply doesn't fit into the new world view? One can only wonder…

Love for Life and Nature

Along our path of Self discovery and personal understanding of love, we eventually come to realize love as an emotion is expressed in countless ways. I first began to understand this when I ventured into Nature and found a deep appreciation for her intricacies. I discovered metaphors, miracles, and infinitely repeating geometry in Nature that helped me begin to uncover the true secret of love that it is not only found in everything we experience, it *is* everything we experience. Love to me has become my architecture of reality itself.

Experiencing my existence in Nature brings me that much closer to my higher Self and in doing so, I begin to see how reality is a precisely woven fabric of the most profound divine frequency. I view that frequency as divine love. I see no separation between Nature and humanity, nor do I see a distinction between what is seemingly physical and that which seemingly can't be touched. Emotion, feeling, intuition, perception and everything else that is seemingly untouchable is also the divine music of love.

But, if hate is an emotion, how can it also be love? If we are all truly innocent, hate is simply an experience for learning no differently than any other emotion. So, if hate is also love, why need we bother ending hate? We really don't have to, however, as I have stated earlier, we must practice love for Self and all being one, we must practice loving Self infinitely. We must practice treating one another the way we truly wish to be treated ourselves and in doing so, the emotion of hate shall pale in comparison to the emotion of love. You see, what I am trying to illustrate here is that love shall prevail because nothing else exists. Emotions are simply experiences that are offered for learning about the archtecture of our reality, the divine music of love.

What I believe is the catalyst for the paradigm shift we are beginning to experience is an understanding that love is universal. Once we each, in our own time, come to realize that we are not separate but rather a thread in the divinely woven fabric, it becomes apparent that we are interwoven with everything in our seeming reality. There is simply no other possibility than for our loving to become universal. Yes, a belief system all the same, but one with profound effects on our world that will deliver a stunningly beautiful and divine experience here on Earth. A harmony that we could only imagine.

Seeing Love As A Gift

Love is a true gift. A life centered on love is one with deeply profound purpose, and in realizing that everything is love, we find a new appreciation for being given this opportunity to experience life. When someone offers their hand in a difficult moment, setting aside their judgement, fear and conditions, the act is a true gift. When we share that love with ourselves, we must cherish and honor that moment also as a gift. When someone selflessly expresses their love we must value the act in epic proportions. When we forgive others, or others forgive us, we must respect the act as a step toward a true understanding of our existence.

I may not always remain focused on the belief that love is everywhere and in everything, but it doesn't make it less true. Being human with an ego that I work to overcome, of course, creates challenges. Living my roles in society, sometimes this truth slips away, but it doesn't make the realization any less valid. A wandering mind is perfectly natural. I believe questioning our existence is exceedingly important, but for me, no matter how much questioning I do, the answer always comes back to the divine music of love.

"Be looking for love. Don't always expect to find it, but grab it when you do." - Thelonious Castaneda

Not the End of the Story

As my perspectives about love have evolved, I've begun to find compassion for all aspects of me, both outward projections and inward truths. This is what balance in this reality is about to me: balancing outward and inward. It is about sharing the experience with those who have agreed to share it with me while maintaining a healthy balance. I try to make decisions based on love, compassion, and forgiveness for myself. Yes, it's the Golden Rule: "Do unto others as you would have them do unto you." The *others* are simply reflections of you. Love yourself both outwardly and inwardly.

My experience with loving myself is a daily practice. Being a giver by nature, I must always keep in check my tendency to neglect my inward Self. However, I struggle because I also am aware that giving to others, when doing so unconditionally, is an act of pure love and light. Serving the needs of those around us is the ultimate service in life, but, as they say, if the airplane is going down, we must provide ourselves the mask of oxygen first. We must be strong enough to help others. We must love ourselves unconditionally before we can extend such an expression to those around us.

As time has passed, I've been rewarded with the true power of finding at least some level of balance between inward and outward love. I've grown stronger. I've become more emotionally secure and confident in who I am and what my relationship with a partner is meant to be. Today, I strive to extend that love to everything in both my inward and outward world. Here is where I have discovered my peace.

I have come to a place in my mind where the people I interact with outside of me are those I have created to help me grow and learn. I now walk among my fellow spirits, standing on my own two feet. The confidence I have always felt in other parts of my life, I now experience in the love of Self.

I have accepted that I have yet to reach a destination on this journey—the finish line I previously thought I had already reached. Life will continue to offer new perspectives, and with them will come new life lessons. Now, for me, it truly is about my rediscovery to the *divine music of everything*.

A Last and First Adventure

I awoke at 8:21 a.m. to the sound of raindrops pattering against my bedroom window. It was a Sunday morning. The August temperatures had dropped, offering a reprieve from the harsh summer sun. It was warm and comforting in bed. I rolled over to see Carrie-Anne snuggled up under the covers. I reached over and moved my fingertips through her hair and down her neck. Her eyes still closed, she smiled and sunk herself deeper into her pillow. It was a beautiful morning.

As I further awakened for the day, I made the decision to take a morning hike in the rain. I love desert storms. The smell of wet creosote, the peace and quiet, and the mist over the rolling mountain ranges all bring me home in the mind.

After gathering my backpack and a light rain jacket, I headed out the door. I made my way in the Jeep down a dirt road en route to one our favorite hiking destinations in the local area known as the Ridgeline flanking the Hieroglyphic Mountains just north of our home.

As the Jeep rumbled along, I began to recall the many hiking adventures Carrie-Anne and I had embarked on over the years to the top of the Ridgeline. We had predominantly hiked the mountain together. I was on my own now, bringing my life full circle.

After I parked the Jeep, I began my ascent to the top. The dark Basalt boulders glistened with rain water. Only an occasional chirp of a camouflaged quail broke the incredible silence. With every step, I could sense the power of solitude returning me closer and closer to my truth.

I paused for a moment, removed my cap, and wiped the sweat from my brow. I gazed out over the desert floor and across the valley to the surrounding mountain ranges shrouded in mist. Raindrops fell all around me. Thoughts twisted through my mind: Can I have my cake and eat it too? *Can I actually allow myself to love me, yet continue to experience and express the outward love of my partner?* I certainly can.

As I reached the top of the ridge to the outcropping where Carrie-Anne and I had shared so many peaceful experiences together, I realized I had once again ascended a mountain for which I could afford myself a 360-degree view of my life. Now, ten years after I selected my first Token Rock from the mountain peaks of the McDowell Range, I was returning home.

I assessed the land around me. To the north were the vast repeating patterns of purple mountains. To the west, my Jeep was a speck among the saguaros scattered about on the valley floor. To the south, I spotted my home, my family, and my societal role in daily life. To the east was the city, and beyond it I could faintly see the McDowell Range some forty miles away. I could make out the peak where I had first discovered my path… where I had found that rock and staked a claim on my life. I was once again in this frame of mind, but things were different now. I wasn't lost. Over the years, I had found myself and had given myself the tools to manage this new growth in life. I was more secure. I had a solid foundation on which I could allow that growth to flourish.

I selected a flat boulder and lay down on my back, facing the sky. There was a steady drizzle still falling. The raindrops fell upon my face and arms like rhythmic notes of Nature's divinity. With each drop, I allowed the emotions to wash away. I expressed love for all things and my Self. I thanked the universe for allowing me to share in this experience. I found solace in the realization that I was whole and complete.

As I descended the mountain, I knew my book was now complete. I could pass it on to the world and allow all aspects of *me* to benefit from its message, and in doing so give myself the true happiness from within that I had always sought: *love for one, love for all.*

"… When we try to pick out anything by itself, we find that it is bound fast by a thousand invisible cords that cannot be broken to everything in the universe. I fancy I can hear the heart beating in every crystal, in every grain of sand, and see a wise plan in the making and shaping and placing of every one of them. All seems to be dancing in time to divine music."

~ John Muir

Quoted in Fox, American Conservation Movement, Page 291

Chapter 8

REDISCOVERING YOUR DIVINE MUSIC

The Keys to a Fulfilling Life

Saving the Music

Looking back on my youth, I can recall many times that music influenced my emotional connection to an experience. Though I didn't think of myself as a musician—mainly because I didn't make learning instruments a priority—I did participate in band, where I played the cornet. My mother's side of the family was very musically inclined. My grandfather had his own band, as did my uncle. I grew up around live music as a part of extended family life.

It was during my high school years that I first became exposed to music in Nature with the writings

I mentioned earlier of Henry David Thoreau, Ralph Waldo Emerson, and John Muir. Their words, which I first read on the pages of a Sierra Club totebook called *Words for the Wild*, offered excerpts of some of their more respected pieces of work. It was in those pages that I first learned about Nature's music, and I was able to relate to what that meant when I spent time in wilderness.

Today, music is a big part of my life in both the form of entertainment and a deep connection to my existence. Without it, I feel as though a big component of this reality would be missing. The grand scale of how music plays a role in our lives is hard to get my arms around, for it is vast. It encompasses all things. As I have often referred to in this book, music at its core is *vibration and resonance*—two descriptive words that represent everything that exists. This is how we appear in form. Music exists everywhere and in everything.

There has been an initiative for some time called "Save the Music." On the surface, the MTV and VH1 generations may see this as simply the need to encourage and support music teaching in schools. This is of utmost importance, but the need for it goes much deeper than a fashionable societal concern.

Music cannot be lost, so there is really no need to save it. However, there is a need to push the cause of remembrance. Music has not lost us, but we certainly have lost it. It is not music that needs saving, but us. Remembering who we are and our deeply profound relationship to the universal language is what needs to be reinstated into our minds. Music is what unites us. It is the foundation of our existence, the key to every seemingly monumental problem this world faces today. It flutters on the wings of butterflies and trickles down the lush green walls of hanging gardens. It can be found in the calculated distances between the sun and the planets and the moments of time from high and low tides. Without it, we do not exist. Listen for it and focus on it, and you will hear it playing as it always has.

There is Only One Language

The human race today speaks a combined total of more than 6,000 languages. Though language is simply the careful placement of tones to formulate words, the words are only powerful if those hearing them can formulate an intellectual meaning to attach to them. The beauty of their meaning can only be appreciated in interpreting their sequence. With so many different languages being spoken in the world today, it is easy to see how language has become one of the key inhibitors to world unity, if not a systematic, organized separation of the masses. If we have effectively individualized and segregated to the point where all we allow for communication is language and there are so many languages being spoken, how can we possibly come to understand each other enough to unify? The answer is music.

There is only one language in all of existence

that makes any difference whatsoever. A quantified understanding of lyrics is not required to establish a unity utilizing it, and music offers such a profound connection that it often provokes emotions that resonate so powerfully with an experience that the music itself becomes exactly what defines the moment. The language we all speak and understand is music.

In fact, music is such a powerful language that it is being used globally to treat and resolve many chronic illnesses. While this may sound like some New Age alternative type of health care, it really is nothing new. Music has been used since the dawn of man to evoke everything from weather patterns to connections with spirit. Nonetheless, there was a time when music was controlled in an effort to cause us all to forget what power it possesses. Having forgotten its power, those who orchestrated the loss used their knowledge of it to control, touting the use of certain notes as the tritone, also referred to in Christian folklore as "*the devil's music*."

Today, a reality is beginning to surface through the research of many qualified experts. The use of sound therapy in Western medicine is slowly being reintroduced.

As was shared earlier in this book, music takes form in all things, from the repeating fractal patterns of the leaves of ferns to the precise architecture of a nautilus. Music can be found in the processes of *earth to earth and dust to dust* and the many creatures that play a role in the cycle of life. By denying a species to survive, we deny one of the many harmonizing instruments to play its tune, and the overall melody suffers for it.

By flooding the crystal streams with human-concocted toxins, we stifle the universal harmony. By dimming the blue skies with a haze of particulates, we create a static that masks the beauty of what plays when we awaken to welcome the morning sunrise. It is without concern for the symphony and the intricacy of each masterfully designed instrument that we fail to remain responsible for how our own actions—those carried out in light of power, greed, and convenience—effect harmony. Thus, we risk being allowed the opportunity to hear it play.

You see, it isn't that the music will stop. It is that we, as a species, may cease to be granted a seat in the orchestra. Mother Nature will prevail because harmony MUST be restored. We have a choice. We have had our solo. Now it is time to sit amongst the instruments and play as one in unity and harmony. We do so through the act of unconditional love. We achieve unconditional love through forgiveness and compassion for our fellow company of instruments—not just human interests but all interests. We must practice harmony.

Music need not be saved, as it exists regardless of us. We simply need to remember who we are, and the music will loudly resonate through our minds, into our hearts, and wrap around us like a warm blanket. Music, the universal language, is love. And as one notable musician poetically stated, "love is all you [and I] need."

How Could this Be Possible?

It will take rethinking about who we are in this experience. Must we seek control? Must we believe that the one ticket we have into eternity is through a higher being, separate from ourselves? Or can we consider, even for a moment, that we have an opportunity to be right now all that we hope to find beyond the veil upon our death. How shall we live this life? We should live as if we were the higher power we seek in divine love. Why would we simply not express now the very characteristics we believe are those of the divine?

I have been deeply contemplating this recently, and I find that the balance between trying to live a life of peace and harmony is a sharp contrast to that of the material world. We awaken each morning, oftentimes with a single goal: to make a living. To achieve goals we believe can only be achieved through expending green paper adorned with little pictures of earlier reflections of ourselves. That very paper that we call currency, though manipulated and concocted into some meaningless form of security features and specialty inks, is rooted in Nature. The trees gave their life, and transferred their energy, so that you could distract yourself long enough to earn their possession (and yes, that goes for the printed version of this book as well!). The reality, on the other hand, is that the trees have already given themselves to you. You need not earn their love, for they give it unconditionally. They shelter you with their shade when the mighty sun casts its harsh light upon your shoulders in the hottest of days. They bare their fruits and offer them to nourish you when you believe your body requires their gifts. They enrich the soil that offers you life and welcomes your physical remains upon your return. Your own body enriches that soil and in turn energizes the mighty tree to once again produce its gifts for those who follow in your footsteps… the future aspects of *you*. And the cycle continues.

It is by incorporating this process into our regular thinking and decision making that we can come to realize what our human physical existence is in relationship our nonphysical existence. We are the energy of the trees and their leaves. We are the sweet, tangy flavor of their juice-filled fruits. We are the worm that bores the hole and the bird that pecks at its bark to bring that worm to its awaiting offspring. We have a place, and that place, though our consciousness seemingly sets us apart, is not one of total control. The control we seek over everyone and everything around us is simply an act of casting that control upon ourselves.

This is not the same as "going green." This is not tree hugging, nor is it a process introduced by "flower children." This is a concept that expands far beyond the borders of these labels. The understanding I share here is one of real love and compassion—a conscious decision as a society to make choices based on balance. If we adhere to this perspective, our existence here may quite possibly be to learn how to release our egos and share in the harmony that is Nature's music—not to conduct the orchestra, but to play along in unison.

Feel the harmony as it weaves its way down the twisting canyon narrows or across the rolling hills of the golden countryside. Discover it resonating from pungent petals of the flowers planted outside your back door. Its presence is not hard to find, you just have to be open to receive it, and there it will be... *your divine music* waiting to be *rediscovered*.

Words of Muir

"...If for a moment you are inclined to regard these taluses as mere draggled, chaotic dumps, climb to the top of one of them, tie your mountain shoes firmly over the instep, and with braced nerves, run down without any haggling, puttering hesitation, boldly jumping from boulder to boulder with even speed. You will then find your feet playing a tune and quickly discover the music and poetry of rock piles – a fine lesson; and all Nature's wildness tells the same story. Storms of every sort, torrents, earthquakes, cataclysms, 'convulsions of nature,' etc., however mysterious and lawless at first sight they may seem, are only harmonious notes in the song of creation, varied expressions of God's love."

~ **John Muir**

(Our National Parks, 1901)

THE MEDITATION CONCLUDES

Time seems to have passed now, but has it? Does time exist, or is it simply a trick of the mortal mind? The call of a raven perched far overhead alerts you to the moment, thus beginning the process of returning you to your physical body.

You turn your attention once again to the powerful energy that is you, sitting atop the granite boulder deep within the canyon. Towering red sandstone cliffs surround you. Long, sweeping stripes of desert varnish flank the walls, exaggerating the expansive height.

The sun shimmers in varying brightness as powdered clouds dance in the sky. With the dimming sunlight, the surface of your skin senses a shift in the divine energy, sending a chill across your arms. The hairs stand at attention like soldiers in a well-choreographed, unified march. Each hair quivers in the breeze as an intricate sensor of perception. As the hairs dance upon your arms, so also do the distant pines standing steadfast upon the rugged outcroppings far above. With the wind, they sway in unison.

You become aware of your surroundings. You question whether what you sense will exist if you open your eyes. Your mind asks of you, *Do our eyes really see, or is it all in the mind? Am I really here? If I am one with all things, how can I ever cease to exist? If I am one with all things, how can I ever fear that which is me? If I am one with all things, how can I ever cause pain and distress to another, since they are simply a reflection of me? How can I ever express anything but love for myself? I judge not, and therefore I be not judged. I hate not, and therefore I must only be love.*

As the sunshine pokes again through an opening in the clouded sky, the warmth blankets your body. You visualize a soft white light cascading down from the heavens as it gently sprinkles the top of your head. The white light flows across your face, down your neck, and rests upon your shoulders. It descends across your chest and the blades of your back, down your spine, and caresses your hips and belly. It continues down your crossed legs and around your feet and toes. As the rays reach the Earth, they penetrate the boulder you sit upon. In a flash of energy, the light surrounds the Earth and unifies you to all that exists upon and within it. It is a love and peace of God that you, yourself, have cast down from the heavens to embrace you.

Your lips speak a whisper into the current of the breeze flowing across your face. Your vocal cords vibrate with a harmony of sounds that blend together into words. *I am one with all that was, all that is, and all that shall be. This is my destiny. It is the destiny of all things seen and unseen. United as one, I am the energy of the tree, the dust, and of the flowing stream. I am the energy, and the energy is God.*

The whispered message blends with the flowing breeze. The energy of the message spreads into infinite oneness with all that surrounds you. As the message expands outward, it catches an uplifting current and reaches into the forest above. As it wisps through the needles of the mighty pine, it delivers the message, and the message is received. It is passed along now not as a whisper, but as a universal knowing—a holographic image of instant oneness. The message is of pure, unwavering love that knows no boundaries, no limitations, no segregations, no judgments, and no fears. It requires no interpretation. It asks nothing in return for everything. It is the universal harmony, and it plays out in each and every moment of our existence. It is a divinity of harmonic resonance that vibrates into form. It is here where we find our Selves. In harmony, we are reunited as one with our divine music, and forever our music shall play.

SELF-IMPROVEMENT RESOURCES

To learn more about Rediscovering Your Divine Music, or the Author, please visit the following links.

Supporting Material: http://www.tokenrock.com/divine_music/
Token Rock: http://www.tokenrock.com
Token Rock on Facebook: http://www.facebook.com/TokenRock
Token Rock on Twitter: http://twitter.com/tokenrock
TruJournal Social Network: http://www.trujournal.com

We welcome your contribution to our website! If you would like to become an offical Token Rock Contributor, please visit us at TokenRock.com and complete our contact form.

How to find Scott:

Scott's Author Website
http://www.scottleuthold.com

Scott's Biography Page on Token Rock:
http://www.tokenrock.com/inspiration/contributor/Scott-Leuthold/3/

Scott's Facebook Fan Page:
@Scott C Leuthold

Step Forward Blog:
http://www.tokenrock.com/blog-Step-Forward-4.html

Seeing Elevens?
http://www.tokenrock.com/explain-11:11-18.html

ABOUT THE AUTHOR

Scott has spent his life as a creative professional, having been nationally recognized for his work in the areas of children's publishing, toys, games, packaging, advertising, and web design.

He is the co-founder of Token Rock, Incorporated and the Webby Award-Nominated website TokenRock.com, an organization dedicated to self-empowerment and personal growth. He writes a blog here about his life experiences titled "Step Forward," as well as numerous articles related to self-improvement.

Scott is also the co-founder of TruJournal.com, a social network community that has become a valuable resource for spiritually like-minded members to share their life journeys through journaling stories and life lessons with others.

He resides in Arizona and travels the world, uncovering the divine music of our existence.

With love to one and all!

Scott

The image shown here, and also on each of the chapter title pages, is a photograph of the original Token Rock randomly selected by the author. This stone represents a milestone that set the course for the organization Token Rock, TruJournal, this book, and Scott's continued exploration and discoveries of life.

If you have a story to share about your own Token Rock, please join us on TruJournal Social Network at:
http://www.trujournal.com

We look forward to meeting you!

JOURNAL ENTRY

Journal Entry: August 2002

I found myself sitting at the top of a mountain today. From home, I hiked up Sunridge Drive toward the foot of the McDowell Mountains a few blocks from home. I hiked up the mountain just west of Copperwynd Resort. I have hiked the McDowells so many times by myself to the top of most of these peaks.

I find that climbing the peaks and sitting at the top alone allows me to really think clearly. The morning was so peaceful, with clear blue skies. I climbed early this morning before the sun had risen over Four Peaks Mountain. It was cool. As I approached the peak and found a comfortable boulder to rest upon, the sun peeked over Four Peaks far off on the eastern horizon. The ray of golden light seemed to penetrate my very being. As I looked down from my perch, I could see the spines of every saguaro cactus below me glowing with sunlight in stark contrast to the shadowed slopes behind them. Early morning—such a magical time of day in the desert.

I closed my eyes and allowed the sun to warm my face. A light, cool breeze blew across my ears. I could hear quails chirping in the distance. As I sat there quietly,

I began to contemplate my life. Am I really happy? What do I really want for my life? Am I willing to take the necessary steps in my life required to paint the picture of my life that I want? I sat there in that one spot for what seemed like an hour in deep thought.

As I rested upon that boulder, I found my hands by my sides, feeling the loose rock beside me. I picked up a rock that fit into the palm of my hand. I lightly rubbed the surface of the rock with my thumb, sensing every contour. As I sat there, something occurred to me. The sunlight on my face, the breeze blowing lightly across my ears, the rock in my hand, and even my own body are all a part of the same thing. The energy of my own body and that of the elements around me have no distinct end or beginning. The decisions I need to make in my life are not unreasonable because tomorrow, the sun will still rise, the breeze will still blow, and the rock in my hand will still exist. My body, my mind, and my spirit – my higher Self – will still continue on. As the thought entered my mind, it penetrated my soul, triggering a release beyond words. All the fear was cast away with the arid desert breeze, dissipating into the countless energetic molecules of the bright blue sky.

Sitting atop that mountain, looking down over the community in which I live, I searched for my home in the maze of streets. I could barely see it down in the valley below;

it was almost microscopic. I realized the world is a very big place with very big processes that keep the big ball revolving. These events seemed much larger than me in that moment, bigger than the trivial issues I experience in my day-to-day reality.

As I considered my life in comparison to the world at large, I realized that I am here on Earth to experience life. If I am not happy on the path I am on, then I can change it. People in my life will survive and adjust. Those around me may or may not understand. I may feel pain in the process, but the pain is worth the energy it takes to live out my life happy.

As I descended the mountain with that rock in my front pocket, I felt a twinge of fear as to what needs to come; but I also realized that living life is not always easy. Achieving happiness sometimes requires tough choices and confidence in yourself that you can get through it. It also requires us to embrace change – not cast it away to the dark corners of our lives.

For me, I shall step up to the plate and take a swing at achieving my goals. I owe it to myself to find my true happiness.

Purpose.
This is what is real, and purpose leads us to love.

~ SC Leuthold